The Veil

The Veil

Heidi Wyrick's Story

JOYCE S. CATHEY AND
REBECCA S. HARRINGTON

iUniverse, Inc.
New York Lincoln Shanghai

The Veil
Heidi Wyrick's Story

Copyright © 2007 by Joyce Cathey

All rights reserved. No part of this book may be used or reproduced by any means, graphic, electronic, or mechanical, including photocopying, recording, taping or by any information storage retrieval system without the written permission of the publisher except in the case of brief quotations embodied in critical articles and reviews.

iUniverse books may be ordered through booksellers or by contacting:

iUniverse
2021 Pine Lake Road, Suite 100
Lincoln, NE 68512
www.iuniverse.com
1-800-Authors (1-800-288-4677)

The views expressed in this work are solely those of the author and do not necessarily reflect the views of the publisher, and the publisher hereby disclaims any responsibility for them.

ISBN-13: 978-0-595-42115-2 (pbk)
ISBN-13: 978-0-595-86488-1 (cloth)
ISBN-13: 978-0-595-86457-7 (ebk)
ISBN-10: 0-595-42115-6 (pbk)
ISBN-10: 0-595-86488-0 (cloth)
ISBN-10: 0-595-86457-0 (ebk)

Printed in the United States of America

In loving memory of our Daddy

Contents

Foreword xi
Introduction xv
1   The Beginning 1
2   The Hospital Stay 8
3   The House on Swint Loop 11
4   Moving In. 18
5   Mr. Gordy 21
6   A Possible Kidnapping 25
7   The Search 31
8   'Con'. 38
9   A Visit To The Doctor 42
10 Calling The Law 45
11 The Revelation 49
12 Searching For Clues 54
13 Smothered 57
14 The Scratches 60
15 The Dark Figure 64
16 Buried Treasure 68
17 Silk Ribbons 71

18	Identification of a Stranger	76
19	The Parapsychologist	80
20	The Study Continues	86
21	Bizarre Occurrences	92
22	A Cry For Help	96
23	The Man In Plaid	100
24	Skeptics	105
25	Unknown Tongues	109
26	Sister Lovie	112
27	Overnight Guests	116
28	Search and Destroy	122
29	Manifestations	125
30	An Unexpected Find	129
31	The House In the Country	134
32	The Uninvited	139
33	Heidi's Private Nightmare	143
34	The Wedding	146
	Epilogue	151
	A Note from the Authors	153

Acknowledgments

First and foremost we want to thank God for his guidance in writing this book. Through his word we have gained knowledge and understanding about things we could not begin to know on our own. And through God, our family has been able to withstand all that has come our way.

We would like to thank our parents for encouraging us to always do our best. They taught us hard work and honesty would take us far in life and that we could accomplish anything we set our minds to. A special thanks to our mother who inspired us with stories from her childhood—stories from a place in north Georgia called 'Hainted Holler' where she grew up.

Thanks to Heidi for allowing us to tell her story and to Lisa for advising us every step of the way to make sure we 'got it right.' Also, thanks to Caroline, Niki and Kelly for proofreading and suggestions.

We extend our sincere love, thanks and admiration to all of our children and grandchildren, and especially our husbands who have stood by us, enduring long hours of writing and re-writing, sometimes neglecting them to meet our goals.

We would like to express our gratitude to three exceptional gentlemen for their assistance in creating our first book: to Dr. William Roll for his countless hours of investigative study and for sharing his insights in the fields of psychology and parapsychology, and ultimately writing the Foreword for this book.; Dr. Frank R. Babish for his valuable knowledge in the field of theology and for his support and guidance; and to Harry Franklin, State Editor of Georgia, our profound thanks for his editorial support and for being a friend. Any mistakes found in this book are ours.

Foreword

When Lisa Wyrick phoned me in 1994 and told about the extraordinary visions of her young daughter, Heidi, and asked if I would help them discover what the reason might be, I called Unsolved Mysteries. The TV documentary had provided funding for other investigations of mine and I hoped they would now do the same so that I could make a personal investigation. Unsolved Mysteries agreed, assuming of course that they could film the study. This was acceptable to Lisa and her husband, Andy.

Unknown to all of us at the time, the show would generate other TV documentaries as well as public appearances by Heidi, Lisa, and Andy. This meant that a large proportion of TV viewers now know about Heidi and her visions. I do not think anyone in the family was happy about the publicity, but it created the need for a book, which the present work fulfills.

To me the book is more important than the TV documentaries. The authors provide a lively and accurate picture of the three main players, Heidi, Lisa, and Andy, all of whom I know quite well. I also know Joyce Cathey, Lisa's sister, and at that time her neighbor, who also played an important part in the story. The four impressed me as straightforward and honest people. I have not met Becky Harrington, the second author, because she lives in Texas. She, Lisa, and Joyce are sisters. Joyce has told me that for the sake of continuity, she and Becky made minor changes of a few facts. The changes are insignificant as far as I'm concerned.

I first thought that extreme magnetic fields in the area might have caused Heidi to experience her apparitions. I have often detected such fields in homes with a reputation of being haunted. The theory seemed plausible, first and foremost because there is a geological fault close to the Wyrick home. Aside from causing earthquakes, which people in the area told me about, subterranean rocks that grind against one another thereby generate electric currents. The currents in turn produce magnetic fields that may extend beyond the surface and affect the brains of people so that they see ghosts and have other odd experiences.

There was a problem with my theory. I tested the Wyrick home and surroundings for unusual magnetic fields but found none. I tried other physical theories but none fit the facts, namely that Heidi correctly described and gave the names of two men who had lived in the area and were now deceased although neither she nor anyone else in her family knew about them. In other words, the girl was psychic. As far as understanding these facts, I came away empty-handed in spite of repeated investigations.

Then I read The Veil and a light went on in my head. I had not been told that Heidi was born with a caul, or veil, over her head, actually the placenta, nor had I been told that she was nearly choked to death by her umbilical cord, which twice encircled her neck. Children who are born with a veil are said to be psychic, but educated people dismiss the idea as naïve superstition. If Lisa had told me that Heidi was born with a veil and that this made her psychic, I would have thought Lisa had lost it.

I have now changed my mind. I am giving a course, "Parapsychology and the Brain," at the University of West Georgia. My main text is a 100-page article on this topic by Dr. Michael Persinger, myself, and two others. Persinger is a well-known Canadian neuroscientist, who has the rare distinction for a mainline scientist of being convinced about the reality of ESP not from books but from his own surveys and experiments. Knowing about Persinger's positive attitude, I brought Sean Harribance, a well known psychic, who has always been ready to offer himself for scientific study, to Persinger's laboratory so that we could explore his brain for factors that might explain his psychic ability (see W. G. Roll, M. A. Persinger, D. L. Webster, S. G. Tiller & C. M. Cook, Neurobehavioral and neurometabolic (SPECT) correlates of paranormal information: Involvement of the right hemisphere and its sensitivity to weak complex magnetic fields. International Journal of Neuroscience, 158, 2002, 197-224.)

The studies that make me feel I understand Heidi's ability are in the section about near-death experiences (NDEs). If a child is born with the placenta covering the nose and mouth this can cause oxygen deprivation, which, as it turns out, may lead to psychic awareness. We do not known if Heidi's placenta covered her nose and mouth, but the fact that she was nearly asphyxiated by her umbilical was clear evidence of oxygen deprivation. In fact she would have died if the cord were not removed as soon as it was.

The neurologist, Dr. E. A. Rodin (The reality of death experiences: A personal perspective, Journal of Mental and Nervous Disease, 168, 1980, 259-263), who has had experienced an NDE himself, explains what happens from a neurological perspective. A serious accident or medical condition causes hypoxia, that is, oxygen deprivation of organic tissue of such severity as to result in permanent change. He writes, "It is known that the earliest effect of hypoxia consists of an increased feeling of well being and a sense of power. This is accompanied by a decrease and subsequent loss of critical judgment" (p. 272). He adds, "Just as in dream consciousness, the patently false is experienced as objectively true." When the condition persists, "delusions and hallucinations occur until, finally, complete unconsciousness supervenes. The loss of oxygen supply coupled with an increase in CO_2 and nitrogen induce a toxic psychosis during the process of dying." From this perspective, the visions of Heidi would have been mere hallucinations. This was far from the case.

Rodin only explains the physiological part of NDEs. In order to include the parapsychological part, we must go to researchers such as Drs. Raymond Moody (Life After Life, Harrisburg, PA: Stackpole, 1976) and Kenneth Ring (Life at Death, New York: Coward, McCann & Georgehan, 1980). These authors tell us that during the NDE, but also afterwards, the person has more ESP than before the NDE and has also more ESP than the average individual.

It seems to me that the most likely source of Heidi's psychic ability is the fact that she was close to death immediately after birth because of being nearly suffocated. We can only speculate about why her ability should only surface several years later. Perhaps anxiety about moving to a new home and neighborhood was the trigger. In any case her two otherworldly encounters occurred shortly afterwards.

There is much more to the story of Heidi Wyrick, but for this you must read the book.

Dr. William (Bill) Roll, Ph.D., Author of several books which includes "The Poltergeist" (1972)

Introduction

This book is based on a true story concerning supernatural phenomena of extraordinary proportions that one family struggled with for more than seventeen years. It is an account of uncontrollable events that caused them undue suffering and despair, and tells of the courage and faith they needed to endure. Although Heidi's story aired twice on national television, she wanted her unusual story set in writing in the event it might enlighten someone else—someone imposed with the same burdens she suffers. This book is not meant to change anyone's opinions, views, or beliefs. It is not meant to turn skeptics into believers. Rather it is about overcoming adversity, overcoming odds, and becoming a better person for it. Heidi wanted her story told and who better to tell it than the family who suffered with her.

1

THE BEGINNING

Lisa had been up all night. A nagging ache began in her lower back after supper last night. She hadn't mentioned it to Andy. She knew he'd overreact, just like he'd done two weeks ago when she'd gone to the hospital in false labor. But as the night wore on the ache became a prolonged, dull pain—an occasional contraction causing her stomach muscles to harden. She couldn't get comfortable. Around midnight she'd slid out of bed and crossed the hall to the nursery. She thought that going through the baby's things would take her mind off her discomfort, and it did for a while.

Now the pain was worse. At two o'clock she decided to wake Andy. The contractions had become regular—the pain in the pit of her stomach more intense.

"Andy." Lisa shook him. "Andy, wake up."

"What is it?" He rolled over and put the pillow over his head.

"I think I'm in labor." A pain hit her hard, radiating from her stomach all the way around to the lower part of her back." Oh, God!" she moaned.

Andy shot out of bed. His Levis and snake boots were donned in seconds. He grabbed his camouflage baseball cap and flung it over his head, turning the bill toward the back. He was ready.

"Let's go!" He grabbed her suitcase from the closet.

"No. It's not time yet."

"What? You know its twenty-five miles to the hospital from here!"

"I know, but the doctor said to wait until the contractions were seven minutes apart and they're just now at ten." She groaned again. Her back was killing her.

"I don't care what he said. We're goin' to the hospital, now!"

She didn't bother to answer. She sat down on the couch, both hands massaging her lower back, her eyebrows furrowed in discomfort.

"I'll tote you to the car if I have to. You know I mean it." Andy paced and worried as he entertained a possible sequence of events that would force him to deliver the baby himself, possibly on a dark, country road with no one around to help.

They heard a loud clap of thunder.

"Alright, I'll call the doctor." Lisa grabbed the portable phone and dialed Dr. Mathew's number. She had to leave a message with the answering service. Within minutes the doctor returned the call and advised her to go straight to The Medical Center—he'd call ahead and let them know she was on the way.

"Come on, let's go."

"I'm calling Momma and Daddy first."

"I'll call them from the hospital. Let's just go!" He was getting anxious.

"No, Andy. It'll only take a minute." She was much calmer than he was.

Before the phone could ring on the other end, she could hear Andy gunning the car engine. He'd left the front door wide open—rain coming in through the screen. He was making her more nervous than the pangs of childbirth.

The drive was horrendous. Reaching the highway Andy stomped the accelerator, pushing the old engine to its maximum output, fishtailing then regaining control. He didn't even slow down for pools of standing water. It was raining so hard they could barely see two feet ahead and lightning was creating an electrical light show in the sky.

The hospital security guard watched as a 1969, canary yellow, Toyota Corolla pulled into a parking space. He motioned for the driver to pull beneath the covered emergency entrance but it was too late. *This must be the couple they're expecting*, he thought.

He was so tired of working the night shift—he was too old for this. He'd retired from the Army in 1981 and worked at the hospital for the last five years. He inhaled a long draw of nicotine and threw his cigarette down, grinding it into the pavement with his boot heel as he watched the young man circle the car and help his wife out. The couple made their way toward the entrance, stepping through puddles of muddy water, pelted by stinging rain. As they approached, he could see that she too, was young—young and extremely pregnant. He was entranced by them for some reason and couldn't help but stare.

The young man had the rugged athletic build of an outdoorsman and his thick, black hair stuck out around the edges of his ball cap, his complexion ruddy from too much sun. The security guard hit the automatic door opener on the sliding glass door. As they entered, he noticed how attractive the girl was, even though her hair hung wet and limp. She turned and looked at him the way you do when you sense someone staring. She smiled and he could see kindness in her face. He nodded at her thinking she had a long road ahead, they both did. He wished them well.

A steady flow of nurses, aides, and family members came in and out of the room. It had been hours, long agonizing hours, since her arrival at The Medical Center this morning, where she was quickly jostled into a wheelchair and rolled up to the maternity ward on the fourth floor. She was dilated to three centimeters.

A full range of medical equipment stood next to her bed continuously spitting out paperwork that recorded the fetal heart rate, blood pressure and other necessary medical information. A wide strap wrapped around her midline monitored the intensity of her contractions. The screen on the cold, steel, robotic machines registered red squiggly lines resembling mountains. When the mountains peaked, her back arched, enduring pain that felt as though it was splitting her in half. Her doctor had advised her to take Lamaze classes—now she wished she had. The medication she'd gotten had done nothing to lessen the pain.

Lisa lay on the hospital bed, her five-foot frame making her appear childlike. Black hair framed her oval face; hazel eyes vigilantly studied the hands of the clock as seconds then minutes ticked by. Morning turned into evening. The blinds were closed but long rays of light peeked through the slits and bounced off the white sheets that covered her legs. She'd dilated to seven centimeters but couldn't seem to get past that. It had been the longest day of her life. Sweat dripped from her long hair and ran down her neck. She was weak and dying of thirst.

She should have delivered the baby by now. She sensed something was wrong. She had an uneasy feeling in her gut. Maybe it had to do with the sudden efficiency of the nurse—her more frequent monitoring of the machines or the way her back stiffened with attentiveness. Visitors were now limited to one at a time.

Now she could hear voices just outside her door, speaking in tones just above a whisper. She had an ominous feeling. The door opened and the doctor walked in—the nurse right on his heels. They both looked grim.

Dr. Mathews broke the news. "Lisa, the baby's in distress." The tone of his voice was sharp.

"What do you mean, the baby's in *distress*?" She started to cry.

Lisa was seventeen years old—she'd led a sheltered life. She had no idea what any of this meant but she knew it was bad. She was scared to death—scared for the life of her baby.

"I think the cord is wrapped around the baby's neck." He looked at Andy. "It is essential that we operate. The cord supplies blood and oxygen to the baby and if it's crimped, any delay could be life threatening." He paused for a moment before continuing. The urgency in his voice was clear. "I'll need you and your husband to sign consent papers and we can go ahead and prep you for surgery."

Surgery! She was stunned. Horrible thoughts flooded her mind as she clung tightly to Andy's hand. She tried to stay strong, but was too weak and exhausted from labor. *All these hours*, she thought, *and now they're going to take my baby by c-section.* She couldn't fight back the tears. *Oh, God, oh God*, she prayed, *God, please don't let my baby die.* She prayed these words over and over. The thought that the baby wouldn't make it was unbearable.

She felt a hand squeeze her shoulder then looked up into the kind face of her doctor. It was a token of comfort as if he was saying, "It's gonna be alright."

Andy was crying, too. He dropped his head into his hands and began to pray.

Within minutes Lisa was being wheeled toward surgery on a gurney. Andy walked fast beside her. The overhead lights streamed past her like yellow lines on a highway at sixty miles an hour.

When they reached the double doors, the surgical tech paused momentarily, "You can say your good-byes here," she smiled at Andy. "Don't worry, she's in good hands. Dr. Mathews is a wonderful doctor."

Andy's eyes never veered from his wife's. "I'll be waitin' right here when you come out." He kissed Lisa gently on her forehead "Don't you worry about nothin'. The baby'll be fine. Just you wait and see." His voice broke up. "We got faith, Lisa. You hold on to that."

"Tell Momma and Daddy to be praying."

Andy stood for a long time gazing toward the surgery room doors after they'd closed. He was worried to death, tormenting himself with disturbing thoughts. He could have been part of the birthing process if it was a normal vaginal birth, but not if it was caesarean. He didn't know if he could deal with that anyway. Even though he was an avid hunter and had gutted many deer, he'd never been able to handle the sight of *human* blood. He began to pace.

The round, steel-framed light on the ceiling above her was blinding. She closed her eyes and felt tears running down the side of her face. She watched the anesthesiologist as he hung the bag of medicine on the pole by her bed and hooked it into her IV in her left arm. The last thing Lisa remembered was the doctor asking her to count backwards—and she did. "Ten, ni ..."

Dr. Mathews took the baby. It was a girl. It was rough going. As the baby emerged he saw a phenomenon he'd only witnessed one other time in more than thirty years of practice. Like a mask, the amniotic sac covered her face and head completely, held fast by strings of skin wrapped tightly around her ears. The navel cord was coiled around the baby's neck twice.

"If this child lives, it will be a miracle," Dr. Mathews announced to the O.R. staff. He unraveled the cord and gently pealed away the amnion sac from her face. He had to work quickly—the baby wasn't breathing.

"Suction!" he commanded. The nurse grabbed the syringe and suctioned her nose and mouth. The baby still didn't breathe.

"Again!" he said, his voice escalating.

The nurse suctioned a second time. Working quickly, Dr. Mathews grabbed the baby by her heels, flipped her upside down and slapped her bottom. When he did, she let out a scream. The doctor breathed a deep sigh of relief and a wide grin spread across his face. She was going to make it. It was times like this that made his job worthwhile.

It seemed like only seconds later that Lisa heard someone calling her name.

"Mrs. Wyrick, wake up. You need to wake up."

Lisa's eyes fluttered but closed again. She was so tired. Where was she? It was cold and she felt herself shiver a little. She was being shaken gently. The words sounded distant.

"Come on, honey." The nurse was persistent.

She realized she must be in recovery now, but her senses were clouded from the sedation. "My baby," she felt the words come from her own lips, but it sounded as though someone else had spoken them. "Is my baby alright?"

The nurse loomed over her fidgeting with the blood pressure cuff. "Your baby's just fine. You've got a little girl—a beautiful little girl with a head full of dark hair. Looks just like her momma."

Relief swept over her releasing a flood of pent up tears. When the tears were spent she fell into a, deep, restful sleep.

Her eyes fluttered open again. This time someone was holding her hand. A tiny, weathered black woman faded in and out of her vision as she fought the need to sleep.

"Stay focused, Ms. Lisa, I got som'in' important ta tell ya."

Lisa looked up—the woman's face was inches from her own. She was staring into the greenest most piercing eyes she'd ever seen, much less on a little dried up black woman. The skin on her face was stretched taut over high cheekbones, green eyes standing out in her black face like a talisman.

"Ms. Lisa, yo' baby done been born wid' a veil on her face. She gonna have powers other folks ain't got and it ain't gonna be easy."

The voice was little more than a whisper.

"Some call'em caulbearers and they's ain't blinded to the other side. Keep yo' eye on her real good, Missy, and don't forget what I done tol' you."

Lisa closed her eyes for a minute and when she looked up the woman was gone. She closed them again and in her mind's eye, she could see those weird, green eyes. She was shaken to the core.

2

THE HOSPITAL STAY

Lisa could hear rain pelting against the window panes as she tried to get comfortable in the hospital bed, turning first one way and then another. They'd had a whole week of rainy, depressing weather. General Beauregard Lee, the Georgia groundhog, predicted another six weeks of cold weather when he emerged from his hole on February 2nd. That was exactly seventeen days before Heidi was born. People in this part of the country trusted the weather forecast of the official doctor of groundology as much as they did the Farmers Almanac. So it'd be safe to say they wouldn't see nice weather again until around the middle of March, at least.

Lisa groaned. She was beginning to feel discomfort in her lower stomach. It should be just about time for her pain medication.

Andy sat in a recliner next to the bed, reared back, feet propped up watching television.

"Andy, can we watch something besides hunting and fishing?"

"This show'll be off in minute. This man just killed an eleven hundred pound brown bear in Alaska. Man! I'd love to do that," he said.

Hunting and fishing was his passion. If Andy had his way, he'd have trophy mounts hanging on every wall in the house.

"I thought you were going to your momma's for supper. She told me she was cooking for you."

"Shoot, you must be crazy. I'm not leavin' you out here at the hospital by yourself. You're Momma'd have a fit."

"Wonder where the nurse is, my stomach's hurting bad." She grimaced. Lisa had a very low pain tolerance.

"Want me to go get her?"

"Somebody should be bringing the baby in here in a minute. I'll just wait."

Lisa was the last of six children, a change-of-life baby. She was brought up as the proverbial 'only child'—her sisters and brothers grown and gone by the time she'd become a teenager. Devout Christians, her parents protected all of them as much as they could from the world—from the sordid details of all that was wrong with humanity. Conservative ideas, actions and habits that had been instilled in them during their upbringing continued in adulthood—and they too, were God-fearing, law-abiding people.

Lisa was brought out of her reverie by a nurse bringing Heidi in.

The nurse laid the small, delicate bundle in Lisa's arms. She was wrapped in a pink blanket, a pink cap stretched over her little head and a beaded bracelet on her arm that read, "Baby Wyrick."

Andy jumped from his chair anxious to hold her—she was only a few hours old. He picked up Heidi's little hand, holding it in his rough, calloused ones. He was amazed that a baby could be this tiny.

Lisa looked at the nurse, "Can you check and see if I can have something for pain?"

"Sure thing," the nurse said, smiling as she left the room.

"She's beautiful, Andy," Lisa said, looking down at her baby daughter.

"Let me hold'er a minute." His eyes glistened.

"Wait a minute. I just got her." Lisa pulled back the baby's hat revealing a tuft of dark hair. Laying the baby on the bed she unfolded the blanket, checking out her feet and hands—making sure everything was as it should be. Satisfied, she wrapped the baby again, swaddling her tightly. She squeezed her gently against her chest for a few minutes before handing her over to her daddy.

Andy was captivated. This little girl would have no problem wrapping him around her little finger. They were smiling like the proud parents they were—their cup runneth over.

A barrage of visitors had been coming and going all day and Lisa hadn't had time to think. It was after they'd left that she broached the subject of the weird incident in the recovery room with the elderly, green-eyed woman. "I really want to find out who this woman is and what she's talking about, Andy."

"You must've dreamed it, Lisa. I've told you that ten times already."

"No I didn't," Lisa was getting mad. "I was wide awake. I could feel her breath on my face—I felt her touch me. So don't ever tell me again that it was a dream."

"Whatever." He said, returning his attention to his daughter.

She didn't feel like arguing with him. She knew what she saw and what she heard and nobody could tell her any different.

Lisa was hospitalized for almost a week because of the c-section. She thought a lot about the woman who visited her in the recovery room and berated herself for not questioning her. She asked every medical person who came in the room about the woman with the green eyes. She was assured over and over again that no such person was on staff here and, as far as they knew never was—that to their knowledge such a person didn't exist.

3

THE HOUSE ON SWINT LOOP

A house is not just a structure built of wood, brick and mortar. Houses become contaminated by those who have lived there before—the walls soaking up memories and feelings as if it were a sponge. Memories of those who may be buried under the soil—emotions of those who fought wars upon the very grounds on which the house was built—memories of people who died there, who loved there, literally seep into their foundations. Good and evil sometimes permeate the very walls of a house, created by hostility, conflict, violence, and evil as well as love and prayers of the ones who had once trod upon the soil.

And so the house on Swint Loop stood waiting—sad, neglected and in disrepair, for a family such as the Wyricks, who, through generations of extrasensory abilities, getting stronger with each generation, to step into its hell hole.

David and Edna, Lisa's parents, discovered the house one Sunday afternoon. They'd been to pick vine-ripened tomatoes at a farm in Ellerslie, Georgia—a farm that had once been an antebellum plantation. When they started home, Edna suggested that they take a different route.

"Turn here," she said, out of the blue, pointing to the road that turned right off Harris Road. They'd been keeping an eye open for Lisa and Andy a place to live but houses in Harris County were hard to find, and expensive to boot.

"Why?"

"I don't know. I've just got a feeling about it."

David didn't question her. He turned right at the sign that read *Swint Loop* and hadn't gone far when they spotted a ranch-style house with a foreclosure sign attached to the front door. The house stood not more than fifty feet from the road. It was empty. From the looks of it, no one had lived there for quite some time.

David pulled the car into the driveway.

Overgrown holly bushes flanked the narrow, concrete front porch and two water oaks lent good shade to the front yard. A flowering quince, rich in red blooms, grew along the property line. The remains of a chain-link fence stood weighted down with a jumble of wisteria and honeysuckle vines. Even though the yard was in extreme need of attention, a colorful pallet of flowers near the front door made it appear *almost* welcoming.

"It looks like it could use a little fixing up," David said, "but hopefully nothing major. I'm gonna take a look around back." He shoved the car in park. Wanna come?" He stepped out of the car looking at the house with a critical eye. He had been one of the top custom-home builders in the area for many years. His black, wavy hair was inherited from his maternal grandmother, a full-blooded Cherokee Indian. He was blessed with a personal magnetism and charm that drew people to him—his green eyes actually twinkling with mischievousness.

He began carefully inspecting the house for termite damage by tapping on the wooden areas and window sills with his pocket knife. It was sound. A few boards were missing from the back deck, some of the window panes would need replacing, and it could use a good coat of paint. But overall the structure itself looked pretty good. He checked the floor joists in the crawl space beneath the house and concluded that the house was worth calling about.

Edna got out of the car and walked toward the thorny quince. She was a natural beauty, her unlined face having no need for cosmetics—light-brown, curly hair still showing no evidence of silver. She was dressed as usual in a simple, A-line skirt and matching blouse. Shielding the sun from her eyes with her hand, she had her first good look at the house. Something didn't feel just right, but she fought off any negative feelings she had about it and focused on how happy Lisa would be here.

The back yard was knee high in weeds. David appeared from behind the house, his pants covered in beggar's lice—small, flat seeds that stick to your clothes like Velcro. He bent over trying to pull them off before he got back in the car—he'd just washed it and it was clean as a whistle. The 1980 Versailles gleamed in the sunlight.

The government foreclosure sign taped to the front door had a telephone number for interested parties to call.

"Edna, I think it looks pretty good. Write down that number and we'll call to see how much they're asking."

From the phone conversation David had with the real estate agent, he learned that the previous owners suddenly abandoned the house—no one knew why. Not surprising though, Mr. Blanton said, everything about those people was strange from what he'd heard. But that was irrelevant. He told David that the house was to be auctioned off by sealed bid starting at thirty-five thousand dollars. David made an appointment for Saturday morning to see the inside.

They arrived at the house ten minutes before the appointment time. A little face was pressed against the back car window as they pulled into the driveway. It was the beautiful face of three-year-old Heidi, eager for the first glimpse of what was to become her new home. As her mom and dad jumped out of the car, their hearts full of anticipation, Heidi held back, physically moving away from the window, as if she felt a strong reluctance to get out. No one noticed the abrupt change in her facial features as she looked up and got the first glimpse of the house on Swint Loop.

It may not look like much right now, but we'll fix it up," David said as he got out of the car. "Come on Andy. Let's look around until Mr. Blanton gets here."

"I love it. It's better than I imagined," Lisa said. Do you really think we could really buy it?"

"I don't know. We'll just have to pray about it," Edna said. "Where's there's a will, there's a way."

"Oh, Momma, Never in a million years would I have thought that me and Andy might have our own house." She was ecstatic.

Regardless of any bad feelings she might've had, Edna liked it. And what she liked most was the location. It was off the main road in an area where there wouldn't be much traffic. She always worried about Heidi having a safe place to play and this house had a fenced-in back yard. Besides that, they wouldn't be throwing their money away on rental houses. It was time to put down roots. They had a child to think about and this place was plenty big enough for the three of them.

A car pulled up and parked behind them. A magnetic sign on the driver's door read *Barfield Realty, The Leader In Southern Home Sales*. A man began unfolding himself from the driver's seat of the small, compact car.

"Howdy folks," he called. "How ya'll doin'?" He reached into the back seat, pulled out a worn, black briefcase and slammed the door shut. He was a large man with short, bristled red hair and a deep, receding hairline. Thick hair grew along the bony ridge above his eyes giving the appearance of one long eye brow.

"Thanks for coming." David walked toward the man and extended his hand. "I'm David Simpson."

They shook hands. "Blanton, William Blanton. My friends call me Bill," his smile showing slightly crooked teeth. "Nice to meet ya'll good folks."

David made the introductions and with that done, Bill gave some history of the house.

"It's been on the market for some time now. I've only shown it to one couple so far. The wife didn't seem to like it much." He dropped his briefcase on the edge of the porch and folded his arms. "Her husband said he supposed she thought it needed too much work." Bill hesitated a moment. "I tend to think there was more to it than that, though."

"What do you mean?" David asked.

"In case you ain't noticed, this area's mostly retired folks who've got nothin' better to do than sit and gab. I understand a rumor got started that a bunch of Satan worshipers used to lived in here somewhere. I think that's a bunch of bull." He paused.

"Look around." Mr. Blanton waved his meaty hand through the air "This is the only house that's been vacated around here in years ... so ... you get my message. When I was showin' the house to that other couple, the misses thought she heard somethin' in one of the back bedrooms. She acted odd—went and sat in the car—acted like she'd seen the devil himself," he chuckled. "Never came back inside. Personally I don't believe in all that mumbo jumbo." He cut his eyes toward David as if waiting for a reaction.

"That does sound strange, alright," David said, all the while thinking about Mr. Blanton's comment about other people gabbing and starting rumors. This man certainly didn't hold *his* tongue.

Mr. Blanton pulled a ring of keys from his pocket and searched the tags for the right one. "Needs a little work, I'd say, but she ain't too bad."

"Daddy can do most of the repairs himself. He's been in the building business all his life," Lisa piped up.

"Me and Chief can do it," Andy added. David was well known around these parts and was always fondly referred to as 'Chief."

"Well, that's real good. Save you a lot of money. I really think this is a great little place." He opened the front door and stepped inside. They all followed.

The inside was in better shape than they'd thought. Knotty pine cabinets in the kitchen were in excellent condition and gave the house a warm, homey feel. The electric stove was an older model, but it would do. The only appliance they would have to buy was a refrigerator.

The carport had been enclosed to make the living area larger. The floor of the den was six inches below the original living area and the concrete floor left bare—it desperately needed carpet. A wood-burning heater sat on a rounded, brick hearth—a hand-hewn, wooden mantle mounted just above it. There were three bedrooms and a bath and a half. It was plenty big enough.

Financially, it would be pushing the limit, but they could do it. Lisa and Andy quickly decided to put in a bid for the minimum amount and signed the contract without hesitation. With the bid submitted there was nothing to do but wait.

A week passed without hearing a word about the house. Lisa decided to call. "I don't mean to bother you, Mr. Blanton, but I'd like to know if you've heard anything?" Lisa was anxious.

"I've not been notified yet, but don't get your hopes up. I don't want to disappoint you but there's no way on earth you'll get that house for the amount you bid."

"Well, I'm not giving up." She knew that property in Harris County was prime real estate, but she also believed that prayer worked. She told Mr. Blanton that her whole family was praying about it.

"Look, Mrs. Wyrick, I've been in this business a long time and I can tell you that houses in Harris County don't come cheap."

Lisa called her mother and told her what Mr. Blanton said. She sounded so dejected that Edna called to up the bid amount. She was told it was too late. Edna felt deep down that there was no need to worry; she just continued to pray.

About a month later David and Edna were at the mall doing some shopping. They were overjoyed when they returned to the car and found that Lisa had left a note stuck under the windshield wiper. It read: *We got the house*! Ultimately their prayers and faith had prevailed.

A few weeks later the Wyricks signed the paperwork making them legal owners of the house on Swint Loop. Sometimes truth is stranger than fiction, as it was this time. It was strange that Edna would intuitively know that they needed to ride down Swint Loop to look for a house—that it turned out their bid was the only one submitted. And stranger still was the fact that they were able to purchase the house for the minimum bid after being assured over and over by the real estate agent that it wasn't possible.

To actually buy a house instead of renting was a huge milestone in Andy and Lisa's life. Who would've thought—one chapter of their life was closing and another one opening. But, as they signed the documents Lisa had a strong feeling of uneasiness.

4

MOVING IN

Packing was almost finished at the house on Denny Road. Andy and Heidi had gone to the new house to see if the electricity had been turned on. Lisa was tired. Her shirt full of dust, a red bandanna tied around her head, she grabbed a glass of iced tea and walked out on the front porch. She needed a breather.

Her mind wandered as she relaxed. Momma was born in a house on this road, probably not a hundred yards from where she now sat. The midwife that delivered Momma, Aunt Mitt, had also lived on this road. In her mind's eye she could see the wagon swaying back and forth—hear the sound of the mule's hooves as they plodded along the dirt road. She could see her Grandma sitting on the wooden bench holding her infant baby Edna. They would have passed within a stone's throw of the house Lisa was moving from—the house where she'd lived when Heidi was born. Her mother and grandmother would've traveled down this same road to their new home in the mountains of North Georgia—to a place called Hainted Holler.

Lisa's heart became heavy with emotion as she realized that four generations—her grandmother, mother, herself and Heidi, had lived in such close proximity, but more than fifty years apart. It was ironic that within hours Lisa would be riding down this same road with Heidi on her lap heading for their new home on Swint Loop.

Jumping up suddenly, shaking off the nostalgia, she went back inside to finish up. After all, this was a happy, exciting day.

The last of the furniture had been loaded and hauled to the new house. In the short time they had been married, they'd moved five times. Moving was no easy chore and hopefully this would be the last time they'd have to do it.

Lisa was able to get the rest of their belongings in her car. She finished cleaning the house and left the keys on the counter. It had been chilly outside this morning but now it was sunny and warm. Indian summer arrived late this year, she supposed, and she'd take that as a good omen. She felt light hearted as she drove down Denny Road.

She pulled into the driveway at the new house and noticed the mattresses were still on back of the truck. Andy was standing in the front yard gazing toward the side of the house as though deeply interested in whatever was going on over there.

"Andy," she called as she got out of car.

"Shhh," he put his fingers to his pursed lips.

"What are you looking at?" Lisa asked as she walked up. He was looking toward the chimney where Heidi was playing.

He turned and gave her an aggravated stare, causing deep furrows to form between his eyebrows. "I'm just wonderin' what she's lookin' at. She's been doin' that all mornin'—just lookin' up at that chimney."

"Well, I don't see anything," Lisa said, following his gaze. She stood there a moment and watched as shadows played against each other, dancing like little fairies on the side of the chimney—hints of evening sun glittering through oak branches. "Heidi, what are you doing," she called.

"Nothing Momma," she ran toward Lisa, wrapping her arms around Lisa's legs.

"You been helping daddy?"

"He won't let me carry boxes. He says I'm too little but I'm not. I'm really big now. I'm almost four."

"Well, you can help me when I unpack, okay?" Lisa bent down and hugged her. You can play a little bit longer if you want."

Turning toward Andy, she said "Come on, we've gotta get the beds together so we'll have somewhere to sleep tonight. I'm beat." She felt as though she could barely put one foot in front of the other.

"'I'll be there in a minute." Several chimney swifts were circling the roof, disappearing into the deep, dark crevice of the bricks. Andy wondered if the birds were what held her attention. "It seems to me like those birds should've migrated by now," he said, making a mental note that they were nesting in there. He turned and grabbed hold the mattress handle.

"Let me help you. I'll get one end."

"I don't need any help. See if you can find the sheets." He easily lifted the mattress over his head—his muscular, well-developed upper arms bulging under its weight.

Over the next few weeks Andy and David repaired broken window panes, replaced planks on the deck and put new locks on the doors. Lisa and her mother worked in the yard and the work made a huge difference in the overall look of the place. Neighbors sat on their porches watching their progress, glad to have people move in who took pride in their home.

Heidi sat on the porch alone, amusing herself as they worked. She sat her small tea set on a makeshift table she created out of empty moving boxes—her doll on one side and her on the other. As she pretended to pour the tea into a small cup, she whispered to Molly, "This house has secrets."

5
MR. GORDY

Heidi would soon be celebrating her fourth birthday. She was a precocious child—blossoming remarkably over the past few months. She was seriously interested in books—in learning to read. In fact, she already recognized words and could write her entire name. She also loved to draw and was beginning to show genuine talent. Her sketches had evolved considerably—far from the stick people she used to draw.

She seemed much older than four, not only in her ability to read and draw, but she could carry on a conversation at a much higher level than most three-year olds. But more than that, assessing other people's feelings or situations seemed to come natural to her and she was blessed with a strong need to comfort.

Heidi was gracious and beautiful and there was something intriguing about her. Everyone loved her—just loved being around her and talking to her. Her dark hair had grown long and hung well below her shoulder blades. Hazel eyes sparkled as she talked about her birthday party.

"Who are you gonna invite to your party?" Lisa asked as she sat down on the couch beside her daughter.

"Me-maw and paw-paw," she said as she concentrated on the picture she was drawing.

"And who else?" Lisa said as she peeked at Heidi's artwork.

"Wolf," she said. Heidi had asked for a dog and Andy brought the puppy home for Heidi right after they moved in—mutual love was instantaneous.

"Wolf? Wolf's a dog. Dogs don't come to birthday parties," Lisa smiled.

"Wolf's my friend."

"Okay, well how about Nanny and Granddaddy? Can they come?"

"Yeah, I want them to come, too." She tore the picture from her sketch pad, eyeing it critically.

"This is for you, Mommy," she handed the picture to Lisa. "Can I go play with Wolf now?" She had the temperament of a normal three-year-old child—she could switch from one interest to another in a flash.

"Sure, but get your coat on. It's cold outside." Lisa got up and hung the drawing on the refrigerator door, moving several other pictures to make room for it.

The holidays came and went without incident. Lisa still had a few boxes left to unpack and she wanted to get that done today. No one could dispute the fact that she had an unusual flair for interior design—she could do a lot with what resources she had. This house was a lot bigger than the one on Denny Road and she kept changing her mind about where her meager furnishings should go.

"Stay in the yard," she warned as Heidi streaked passed her dressed in her blue coat and toboggan. She could hear the weather broadcast from the radio. A computerized voice predicted mostly sunny skies—highs in the mid fifties, northeast winds around ten to fifteen miles per hour—lows tonight around thirty-eight degrees. Today would be a typical winter day in southwest Georgia.

Heidi stepped out into the morning air and looked around. She didn't see the puppy anywhere.

"Come'er Wolf," she called.

"Here Wolf. Come'er boy," she tried to snap her fingers like she'd seen her daddy do, unaware that they made no sound.

Wolf usually came running with his tail wagging the second she stepped outside, but this time he didn't. She checked the doghouse.

"Where are you Wolf?" She walked around the yard.

She thought she heard a 'yip' coming from under the house. She moved toward the deck, getting down on her knees to peer beneath the wooden planks.

"Wolf?" She saw yellow eyes peering from out of the darkest corner.

"Hey, boy," she said in the special tone of voice she reserved only for Wolf. "There you are. Come on, Wolf," Heidi coaxed, but Wolf wouldn't budge. The more she called, the deeper into the shadows Wolf shoved—scratching up dirt with his hind legs as if to bury himself. She reached her hand toward the dog and he snapped at her tiny fingers. A low growl erupted from his throat and his ears stood up at attention—the thick fur on the back of his neck bristled. Wolf was scared.

Sensing someone was there, she turned slightly. She could see a pair of black, shiny shoes right next to her. She stood up brushing dirt and grass from her hands, and then stared up at the tall figure of a man.

"Hello, Heidi," a deep voice said.

Heidi stared at him.

"Your name is Heidi, isn't it?"

"Yes sir and I'm this many," Heidi held up three tiny fingers, "but I am almost four." She smiled big.

"Well, my name's Mr. Gordy and I use to live around here." He paused. "I have a swing on that old tree over there," he pointed next door.

"You do?" Her eyes lit up at the mention of a swing.

"Sure do, and if you want, I'll show you sometimes. You like to swing?"

"Yes."

"Maybe when I come back, I'll let you swing on it. I'll push you real high," he smiled.

"That'll be fun." She brimmed with excitement. "But, I have to ask my momma."

"It's alright, Heidi. You don't have to be afraid of me. I won't hurt you. I'm not a bad man. I just want to be your friend," he said reassuringly.

"I wanna be your friend, too." Heidi paused briefly. "You know what Mr. Gordy, I got a puppy. Wanna see him?" Heidi squatted down and called Wolf again and when she stood up Mr. Gordy was gone. As quickly as he appeared, he was gone, vanished into thin air.

"Mr. Gor-deee," she called, but he didn't answer. "Mr. Gordy, where are you?" Childlike, she looked around wondering where her new friend had gone. But shortly, she turned her attention back to Wolf.

Instantly and unconsciously her decision was made. She trusted this man. In those short moments on that cold February morning in 1989, a bond was established between Heidi and Mr. Gordy that would last a very long time.

6

A Possible Kidnapping

Lisa glanced at the antique clock she'd hung over the mantel in the den and realized it was almost lunchtime. Heidi had been outside for a while but she checked on her daughter often. Realizing Heidi would be hungry by now, Lisa hurried into the kitchen to fix a quick lunch for both of them.

She opened the door to call her, but Heidi was already crossing the deck toward the back door. "Hey, you hungry?"

There was a striking resemblance between Heidi and her mother. It was uncanny the way people looked at the picture of Lisa at three years of age and automatically thought it was Heidi. Both had long, dark hair that fell to their shoulders and striking hazel eyes framed with long dark lashes. Maternal genetics were definitely dominant in Heidi's appearance, Lisa bearing a strong resemblance to *her* mother.

"Momma, Wolf was hiding," Heidi said as she took her coat off and flung it over the back of her chair.

"Did you find him?"

"Yeah. He was under the deck."

"Well, I'm glad you found him."

Lisa grabbed the bread and peanut butter off the pantry shelf and made them both a sandwich. She looked at her daughter thoughtfully as she ate. She sensed something was wrong.

"Is something bothering you, Heidi?"

"No ma'am."

She laid her half-eaten sandwich on the plate, "Momma, I got a new friend today."

"Are you talking about Wolf?"

"No, he's a man."

"What are you talking about Heidi? Nobody's been here."

"Uh huh. His name's Mr. Gordy and he's nice. He said he'd push me on his swing." She was smiling. "I said I have to ask my momma first," Heidi boasted, remembering her mother's warnings about strangers.

"Did he say anything else to you?" Lisa looked apprehensively at her daughter.

She thought a minute. "He said, 'I'm not bad'."

"Heidi Wyrick, what have I told you about talking to strangers?"

"I like him, momma. He said he's not gonna hurt me."

"What'd he look like?" Lisa was feeling a little uneasy.

"He's old, real old and got white hair." She smiled. "I like his white hair. I wish my hair was white like Mr. Gordy's." Heidi stroked her own dark hair with her tiny fingers then reached for a cookie.

"Listen to me, Heidi. This is very important. I need to know what this man was wearing." This was sounding too real.

"He had on a big hat, but not like Daddy's." Heidi reached a tiny hand high over her head extending her fingers to length.

"Did he have on blue jeans?" She watched her daughter closely.

"No. He had on a suit like Daddy wears to church, but it was black."

Heidi had never made up things, Lisa thought. *No, no. Too much detail; way too much detail for a three-year-old. Someone was out there with her. A man named Gordy. She didn't know any Mr. Gordy.*

Lisa's neck had tensed up. Had someone tried to abduct her daughter from her own backyard, from right under her nose? Surely not. Not as often as she walked back and forth checking on Heidi. She would have noticed a strange man.

What should she do? *Think Lisa*, she told herself. *Just stay calm and think this out.* There'd been a rash of kidnappings sporadically around the United States lately, but every one of them had been in large cities.

None had happened in small towns like Ellerslie. But until she found out differently she'd have to treat this seriously. Her young, innocent daughter could've been snatched away in an instant and never seen again.

Lisa got up from the table and put her arms around Heidi. She thanked God for keeping her safe. Her hands were visibly shaking as she reached out and turned the dead bolt on the back door. She never locked the doors during the day—she'd never had any reason to. She peered through the curtains, her eyes sweeping the yard and up and down the two-lane road. Nothing seemed out of the ordinary.

She pulled the curtains tight. Anger began to mount. *If that man has the gall to come back to this house he'll have a surprise waiting for him*, she thought as she bolted across the den to Andy's gun cabinet. She grabbed hold of the door. It was locked! *Where did he hide that stupid key?* She ran her hand along the top edge of the cabinet but didn't find it. She suddenly realized that if she found a gun she had no idea how to load it, much less shoot it. She knew she was overreacting but she couldn't help herself. She'd never been in a situation like this. For the first time, she desperately wished she'd accepted Andy's offer to teach her about guns. Her only child could be missing right now and her protective instinct was totally controlling her.

She watched as Heidi crossed the floor to stand by the heater. *What nerve this Mr. Gordy had!* She grabbed a knife from the kitchen drawer. She ran her finger along the long, sharp blade. It would do! She shuddered at the thought of having to stab somebody, but to protect Heidi, she could do it. A mother's love certainly knows no bounds. She had first-hand knowledge of this now.

I shouldn't have let her go outside alone, she thought. *I should've kept a closer eye on her.* She tried hard to rationalize it. *Don't be silly. You can't make a child play inside the house day in and day out.*

She knew she was beating herself up over this and she shouldn't. But still, in her worst nightmare, she couldn't imagine losing Heidi. In a single instant she could have been gone. One thing for sure, her baby wouldn't end up a statistic if it was within her power to prevent it—she'd never be able to live with that.

Heidi, oblivious to any danger, picked up her sketch pad and pencil and began to draw.

Lisa glanced at the clock again, paying little attention to what Heidi was sketching. She wanted to call Andy. She needed him to come home. He worked as a truck foreman for the county and spent most of his day driving lengthy routes in rural areas. She knew he probably wouldn't be back at the office. It was only twelve-thirty. But she'd give it a shot anyway.

The telephone beeped loudly in her ear. She nearly jumped out of her skin, but sighed with relief when she realized the off-the-hook alarm had been activated. How long had she been standing there with the phone turned on? Stress overload had caused her mind to go totally blank. She couldn't remember Andy's work number—her fingers began drumming the outer edge of the phone. She remembered writing the number down on something but for the life of her, she couldn't remember what. She rummaged through the kitchen drawer for the phone book. Quickly thumbing through the pages, she found the number.

A secretary at the county office answered the phone.

"Hello, this is Lisa Wyrick, Andy's wife. I need to get in touch with him right away. It's sort of an emergency."

"Hold on a minute. I'll check and see if he's here. I think he may be out there switching out his truck."

A few minutes later she heard Andy's voice, "Hello."

Lisa couldn't speak.

"Hello, this is Andy."

"Andy, it's me. I need you to come home." She knew she should try and stay calm.

"What's the matter?"

"There was a man in the backyard talking to Heidi. I'm terrified that he was trying to kidnap her."

"What? Kidnap her? What are you talkin' about, Lisa?" the volume of his voice began to escalate as panic set in.

"She said a man came in the backyard and offered to play with her—said something about a swing. But she's okay. She's sitting right here in the living room with me."

"I'm comin' home." Andy slammed the handset down onto its cradle.

"Drive safe," Lisa muttered under her breath. Maybe she shouldn't have been so abrupt over the phone. She knew he'd literally fly—something else to worry about now. She shook her head.

She sat close to her daughter. Heidi had turned on the TV and was singing along with Barney, *"I love you, you love me, we're a happy family..."*

Lisa picked up the remote and turned down the volume. "Heidi, I want you to think real hard. This is very important. You know the man you met in the backyard today?"

"Yeah, Mr. Gordy."

"Have you ever seen this man before?"

"No ma'am," Heidi said, "But he promised me he'd come back. He promised to push me on the swing."

Stunned, Lisa was unable to go on with her questioning.

He promised me he'd come back. Chilling words.

No use questioning her further. She turned the volume back up. Barney was still singing and Heidi joined in. Lisa picked up the sketch pad Heidi had been drawing on. It was in rough form, of course, but it looked like a man. Lisa thought nothing of it—Heidi was always drawing pictures of the family. She tossed the pad back onto the coffee table, unable to think about that right now.

Fear was not good, but on the other hand, having no fear could be even worse—and Heidi had no fear of this strange man and that's what disturbed her most.

Lisa lifted Heidi onto her lap. She held her close and breathed the scent of her hair, feeling the softness of her skin. Heidi was her joy.

Since the day she was born Lisa had a deep seeded fear that something might happen to her. She guessed it was because they almost lost her at birth. She thought a lot about the Bible scripture, Job 3:25. It says, "For the thing which I greatly feared is come upon me, and that which I was afraid of is come unto me." That was a terrifying thought. She tried to pray. Now she was extremely frightened.

7

THE SEARCH

Although it seemed like hours since Lisa had called Andy, only ten minutes had passed when she heard the familiar sound of his truck engine as he turned onto the narrow road connecting their house to the main highway.

Heidi jumped from her mother's lap and picked up a toy train engine lying on the floor next to the coffee table. "Momma," Heidi said, handing Lisa the toy. "Can you make this work?"

"I think the batteries are dead, honey." Lisa flipped the switch several times—nothing happened. "We'll have to get new ones."

She handed the toy back to Heidi and walked to the front door to look out. Andy was pulling into the drive. He turned so quickly the truck slid to one side of the road, leaving black streaks on the asphalt. The truck came to an abrupt stop near the house and Andy jumped out leaving the truck door ajar.

"Where's Heidi?" he blurted as he stepped through the front door. Anger consumed him as he drove home—anger that a strange man entered their fenced yard and talked to his three-year old daughter. He had to be up to no good.

"Here I am, Daddy!" Heidi said, fumbling with the switch on the train.

Andy gathered his daughter in his arms and squeezed her gently.

"Daddy, can we get new batteries for my train? It won't work."

"Okay. The next time I go to the store I'll get you some." He managed a smile. "I need to speak to Momma for a minute. I'll be right back." He sat Heidi down and started toward the kitchen, Lisa trailing behind.

She grabbed the coffee pot as Andy reached for his mug. Lisa began to explain everything that had happened, careful to convey Heidi's exact words.

Andy's face was a splotchy red. He began pacing the floor—furious and agitated. He pulled a can of Copenhagen out of his jeans pocket and pinched out a wad, shoving it into his jaw with a vengeance. He couldn't stand still. He felt as though his head would explode. Before Lisa could finish he headed for the gun cabinet in the corner of the den, reached high above it, and retrieved a key from beneath an ivy-filled planter. Lisa watched motionless as he unlocked the case, making a mental note of where he kept the key. He removed a double-barrel shotgun, grabbed a hand full of shells from the bottom drawer and dropped them into the pocket of his blue denim jacket. Slinging the strap of the gun across his left shoulder, Andy headed for the front door.

"Let's just call the police," Lisa said worriedly. She never should have said the word "kidnap."

Andy's tone was subdued. "No. I'll handle this myself and that's all there is to it." He turned to Lisa. He wanted her full attention. "If I find this Mr. Gordy, I'm gonna kill'em," he announced—veins protruding at his temples. "Keep the doors locked while I'm gone and don't open'em for anybody." He slammed the front door.

Lisa paced the floor fretting about Andy, worrying about Heidi. Why hadn't she called the police when it first happened? She wasn't thinking straight. What would Andy do if he found this Mr. Gordy? He'd probably put a bullet between the man's eyes instead of asking questions, that's what. He could display a violent temper when it came to the safety of his wife and daughter.

Her mind and thoughts were in turmoil. The man could be innocent but it sure seemed odd that he appeared in their yard and spoke to no one except Heidi. Why hadn't he come to the front door? Why'd he go around back through the gate? No—something didn't feel right. This man was certainly up to no good. *Maybe Andy outta shoot'im,* she thought. *That'd serve him right.* Terror coursed like an icy river through her veins. If he found the man, Andy's temper would probably land him behind bars before morning.

Andy began his search on the other side of the narrow road, asking his new neighbors questions about the gray-haired man Heidi had described so vividly to her mother. She'd never lied to them before and he had no reason to believe she had now. No, she definitely had a visitor today and that visitor was in a heap o' trouble. He knocked hard on the screen door of an old wood-frame house and an elderly man appeared.

Hobbling slowly across the porch the man asked, "What can I do for ya?" He pushed open the screen door. He looked kind, his brow furrowed with age—the knees of his denim coveralls worn thin.

"Afternoon, Sir. I'm Andy Wyrick. We just moved in that house over yonder." Andy spit a wad of tobacco juice on the ground then pointed toward the house across the road. "I'm lookin' for a man named Gordy. Don't know his first name."

"Gordy ... Gordy," the old man repeated as he moved down the steps. "I don't recollect anyone by that name, and I've lived 'round these parts for pert' near ten years." He shook his head. "I'm sorry son, but it just don't ring a bell. By the way, name's Thomas J. Jackson, named after Stonewall. You can call me Tom." The old man's head was bobbing around like a fishing cork, iron-gray spirals of hair sticking out like bent corkscrews.

Andy sighed. "Well, thanks anyway, Tom. If you see any strangers hangin' around, I'd appreciate it if you'd call me." Reaching inside his coat pocket, he found a pen and an old gas station receipt. He scribbled down his phone number and handed it to his neighbor.

"Sure thing" Tom said. The old man reached out an arthritic hand taking the paper from Andy, slipping it into his pocket. "What's this

Gordy feller gone and done, if you don't mind my asking?" He looked curiously at Andy.

"He's been messin' with somebody he shouldn't have," Andy turned toward the old man, a steel glint in his eye. "I gotta go now, but like I say, I'd be mighty thankful if you'd call me."

As Andy turned to walk away he heard the latch click on the old screen door. Then he heard the old man say, "Can't be too careful this day in time." Until then he hadn't thought of how he must've looked with that gun strapped over his shoulder.

Andy had been to practically every house in the small neighborhood but had only spun his wheels. Nobody could give him any information on this Mr. Gordy nor had they noticed any strange men hanging around. Some of the neighbors looked at Andy as if *he* might be dangerous, and understandably so. Fury had given him the appearance of a mad man, eyes burning with intensity—head and neck red from anger. He'd be lucky if they didn't call the cops on him. *Well let 'um*, he thought. He was still fuming, *some pervert messing around with little girls outta be shot.*

Dusk had moved in; the sky red above the horizon. When Andy looked up at the evening sky, something in the far reaches of his mind surfaced. It was something his grandpa used to say, "*Red skies at night, sailors delight.*" It wouldn't rain tonight.

A cool northerly wind blew. He'd lost track of time—he was tired. He didn't want to give up the search, but all his efforts proved futile. He felt weak from hunger and the initial surge of adrenalin had disappeared, leaving him drained and discouraged. He hadn't eaten since breakfast, and Lisa would soon have dinner ready. It was getting late—a pale sun hovered above the tree line in the distance. Disappointed and weary, he shouldered his gun and trudged back to the house.

Andy, a product of generations of southern breeding, inherited the genteel attitude towards family, and a steel-infused determination to protect them at any cost. Mr.Gordy was a walking dead man.

Lisa was anxious. She watched the clock as minutes slowly ticked by. Heidi had been in her room for a while now and Andy had been gone for hours. She struggled with the idea of calling her momma and daddy. She didn't want to worry them but it always seemed as if the battle was already won once they found out. Her parents were very protective of all their children. She worried about her daddy's temper though. He was raised during the depression in a family of fifteen, learning early to use a weapon to get what they needed to survive. Her daddy wouldn't think twice about hunting this man down—that is if Andy didn't find him first. But on the other hand she needed to talk to someone. She finally reached for the phone and called her momma.

Just talking with her mother and sharing her burden, seemed to expel some of her fears. "Be careful what you say to Daddy," she said, just before hanging up. "You know what a temper he's got."

"I will," her mother promised. "But you be sure and lock those doors. Call me as soon Andy gets back."

She placed the phone on the base and began to pace back and forth, praying Andy would be back soon.

Her thoughts were suddenly interrupted by a vaguely familiar sound coming from the back of the house—she couldn't quite place it.

"What's that noise?" she called out to Heidi.

"It's my train," she heard Heidi say.

"It can't be. The batteries are dead," Lisa said, as she opened the door and stepped into Heidi's room. Scooting across the carpet was the little engine—its little wheels turning—its whistle blowing.

She heard the front door open and close. "Is that you, Andy?" She ran toward the living room where Andy was already returning his Remington to the gun cabinet. He didn't answer. Just one look on his face and Lisa knew his search had been futile.

"I'm so glad you're finally home." She put her arms around him. "You didn't find him did you?"

"No." He pushed her arms away, walked over and dropped onto the couch, disgusted and discouraged. "Hear me out on this, Lisa. This neighborhood only has one way to get in and one way to get out. Shorty's store is right at the top of the hill and he knows everything that goes on. He's says he ain't seen no stranger—not even a strange car. Nobody around here's seen a thing. Is this man Houdini, or what? How'd he get here, walk? I don't think so. We live too far out." Andy ran his hand through his thick, prematurely graying hair. "He'd have to have a car, so where was it? There's absolutely nothin' says some pervert's been hangin' round here. On the other hand, I don't believe Heidi would tell a lie. This is frustratin' as all get out."

Lisa knew Andy was frustrated; she was too. He looked worried, frightened. Part of her wanted so badly for Andy to find the man—but, part of her was afraid for Andy. But somehow, something inside her told her he wouldn't find an answer.

"Don't let Heidi outta your sight Lisa—not 'til we can figure this thing out." He lowered his head into his hands.

"You don't have to worry about that." Lisa slipped her arm around Andy and squeezed him tightly.

Lisa watched Heidi as she played. She was absorbed in her own little world—unconscious of the danger she'd encountered earlier that day. She glanced back at Andy.

"Did you, by chance, put new batteries in that little toy engine Daddy bought for Heidi?" She knew he hadn't, but she felt the need to ask anyway.

"No. We ain't got any batteries."

"That's what I thought, but just before you got home that train was rolling across the floor whistling."

"What are you saying? That thing can't run on air!"

Lisa ran to the bedroom and grabbed up the train and flipped the switch back and forth—the wheels didn't roll—there was no sound.

She opened the battery compartment—it was empty. A feeling of foreboding made her chest feel tight.

The whole day had been strange. It had gone from a possible kidnapping attempt to trains running on nothing but thin air. *I must be losing my mind*, she thought. Lisa looked out through the bare glass panes of the kitchen door. The night was as black as pitch—only a sliver of a waning moon could be seen through the trees. She felt herself shudder.

8
'CON'

There is a world we cannot see. Battles rage in that dimension—good against evil—angels against demons. This has been so since the beginning of time. Few among us have been chosen and are able to see into other dimensions. Among the chosen is Heidi Wyrick. She was born with this gift—this awful sensitivity to human spirits that lurk beyond the grave.

Heidi was growing up fast. According to the pencil marks on the door jamb, she'd grown a whole inch in the last six months. She prided herself in the fact that she stood much taller than her cousin, Brooke, even though Brooke was more than a year her junior.

"Stand still," Heidi instructed as she slid the pencil across the top of Brooke's head, marking a spot much lower than the one her dad had made for her just yesterday.

Brooke wiggled from beneath Heidi's arm, clearly not interested in her height at the moment. She was more interested in the funny-shaped round thing with a thin, metal strip bearing numbers—a thing that seemed to have no end when she pulled it from it's sheath.

There was a soft rap ... rap ... rap ... at the front door. Heidi flung the pencil onto the counter. Rap ... rap ... rap ... There it went again.

"Momma, somebody's at the door," Heidi yelled. She heard the drone of the vacuum cleaner coming from the back of the house. "Momma!" Lisa didn't answer.

"Brooke, go get Momma."

Brooke paid Heidi no attention at all. She just stood there dawdling with the tape measure, pulling it in and out and letting it zip backwards into its casing.

Rap ... rap ... rap. Heidi started toward the front door but hesitated for a moment. She had been warned time and again since her first meeting with Mr. Gordy to be cautious and not open the door for anyone. But the knocking was persistent.

She pulled the door open. Standing outside the screen door was a man. The first thing she noticed was a bloody bandage on his left arm which he held protectively against his chest. He was clothed in a pair of khakis and a white tee shirt that was covered with blood.

"Are you alright, Mister?" Her eyes slowly moved up from the wounded arm to the stranger's face.

"I am now," he smiled.

Heidi didn't feel threatened. The only thing she felt was compassion.

"How'd you get hurt?"

"It was an accident that happened a long time ago."

He stepped a little closer. "My name's Con. I've been waiting a long time to talk to you."

Blood oozed from the tattered bandages that were wrapped loosely around his arm. Heidi was alarmed.

"Just a minute. I'll get Momma," she spun around and took off. "Momma!" Momma! Come quick. Con's hurt."

Lisa pulled the vacuum cleaner cord from the wall as Heidi grabbed her hand.

"Hurry!" She said frantically.

Heidi ran back to the front door—Lisa hurrying behind her. Sunlight streamed through the empty portal. Con was gone.

That night after Brooke had gone home and Heidi was finally in bed, Lisa began to reflect on the eerie events of the day. She felt a stab of anxiety as her thoughts flashed back to the first day Heidi talked to the man she called Mr. Gordy more than a year ago. Was Con and Mr. Gordy the same man? Perhaps "Con" was his first name and Gordy his last. *That must be it*, Lisa thought. But why did Heidi describe him differently? Now, instead of a black suit and hat, he was wearing a white tee shirt tarnished with blood stains. Lisa felt totally bewildered. She was tired of hearing about this strange Mr. Gordy. And now she's hearing about a man called Con. *What next,* she thought.

Lisa pulled back the covers and slid between the sheets. Andy crawled into bed next to her and rolled his pillow under his head. He'd just gotten home and it was late. He'd been out at his hunting lease searching for a good place to mount his deer stand and this was the first chance she'd had to talk to him.

"It's starting all over again."

"What's startin' over?" He picked up the remote control and flipped the TV to the eleven o'clock news.

Lisa took the remote from his hand and switched off the TV. She needed to get this off her chest.

"Heidi's talking about that strange man again, only this time she's calling him Con. Said he knocked on the front door today and when she couldn't get my attention she opened it herself." Lisa continued to fill Andy in on the details. "Last time she called him Mr. Gordy, now she calling him Con. I just don't know what to make of it!"

"And where were you?" Andy asked accusingly.

"Vacuuming," she snapped back. She didn't particularly like the tone of his voice. "I didn't hear a thing until Heidi came running asking me to help him. When I got to the door there was nobody there. She was adamant about it, though—swears the man was there."

"That don't make a bit of sense, Lisa." He cleared his throat.

"I know, but that's what she said."

"So you're tellin' me that a man came to our house with blood all over him and you didn't call anybody?"

"I didn't know what to do, or who to call. You and Daddy were at work. Anyway, by the time I got to the door, he was gone."

"That's plain crazy. I'm startin' to think she's makin' things up."

"What if she didn't make it up? What if it's true?"

"I don't know what to do, Lisa," Andy was silent for a few minutes. "This whole thing's puzzlin'." He threw the cover back and sat up on the edge of the bed. "I said this once and I'll say it again, if I find somebody snoopin' around here, there'll be hell to pay. I ain't playin'."

Lisa turned over and faced the wall, immersed in her own thoughts. She knew her child. She didn't believe Heidi would make up such a companion, let alone one that was injured and dripping with blood. She'd been so sincere, so blatant about it, when she'd mentioned it. First he mysteriously appears to Heidi in the back yard. The next time he shows up at the front door. *If this sort of behavior continues*, she thought, *I'll have to call her doctor.* This just didn't sound normal.

9

A Visit To The Doctor

Lisa had taken a part-time job at a local print shop after Heidi started Pre-K in the fall. She didn't feel comfortable about leaving Heidi in an after-school program so she made sure she was always there when school let out. Heidi spoke of Mr. Gordy often. Sometimes she called him "Mr. Gordy" and other times she called him "Con." Lisa was forced to accept it. Mr. Con Gordy had become a household name. But what was disturbing was that Heidi was spending more time in her room. Although much of that time was spent reading or sketching, she insisted that Mr. Gordy visited her there and that's what worried Lisa most.

The more time Heidi spent alone, the more troubled Lisa became. She eventually decided to make an appointment with Heidi's pediatrician. She and Andy were concerned enough to discuss the on-going problem with a professional.

After the examination, the doctor talked to Lisa and Andy privately. He laughed as he assured them that it was healthy for children to have imaginary friends. He explained that as children grew older and made more friends that it was likely their imaginary ones would disappear.

"What a relief," Lisa said with some resolve as they drove home. But even as she spoke, doubt still lingered. She was bothered about the fact that the imaginary friend was not another child. Why had she chosen an older man for a companion? This just didn't make sense. There was something to be said about a woman's intuition.

"I told you it was just her imagination," Andy said. Moments later he burst into laughter.

"What's so funny?" Lisa asked.

"You know. I was just thinking about how ridiculous I must've looked that first day Heidi told us about Mr. Gordy. Here I was stalkin' the neighborhood with a shotgun lookin' for somebody who didn't even exist. Boy that makes me feel stupid."

Heidi sat quietly in the back seat, listening to her parent's conversation. She was old enough to understand what the doctor said. He said she made things up—said Mr. Gordy wasn't real. *He was real—real as anybody else—and Con was real, too*, Heidi thought, as she gazed out the window. She told her momma and daddy she didn't make it up. Why didn't they believe her instead of the doctor?

The alarm clock didn't go off again and Lisa overslept. She woke Heidi and then jumped in the shower. When she got out, Heidi was already dressed and sitting on the edge of her bed. She uncoiled the cord to the blow dryer and plugged it in.

Lisa shivered. *Why was it so cold in here all of a sudden?* she thought.

"Is it cold in here to you Heidi?" she said, rubbing her arms.

Heidi wasn't listening. Her eyes were focused on something directly behind Lisa's left shoulder and from the look on her face, Lisa knew something was wrong.

"What is it Heidi?" she was afraid to turn around.

"There's a man right behind you." Her tone was very quiet.

Immediately a voice popped into Lisa's head, "*Mr. Gordy promised he'd be back.*"

"Is it Mr. Gordy, Heidi"? She still hadn't turned around.

"No. Mr. Gordy is not black."

"Lisa was afraid to turn around, but she did; she had to.

"Heidi, nobody's in here. Don't do that to me again!" Lisa scolded. "You nearly scared me to death."

"There was a man there Momma, cross my heart and hope to die," making the gesture of crossing her heart with her finger.

"Have you seen this black man before?"

"Yes, I think he likes your bedroom."

"Lisa felt like she might have a panic attack. "Come on Heidi, let's get out of here."

She buckled Heidi in the back seat of the car and got in on the driver's side. She sat there for a few minutes just holding on to the steering wheel.

Heidi had scared the pure hell out of her, but putting that aside, why hadn't *she* been scared? Lisa didn't understand it. *What was it about this child*, she pondered. As her heart rate slowed a bit she began to think more clearly. She loved Heidi dearly. She was her child, her only child. She was beautiful and bright and had the charisma she'd not seen before in a four year old. She was different, that's all, and she would have to accept that.

10

CALLING THE LAW

Lisa hadn't rested well in days, especially since Heidi's claims of seeing an injured man at the front door and the black man in her bedroom. Her sleep had been inundated with nightmares. Night after night she dreamed about unidentifiable creatures darting in and out of her bedroom and about Heidi being dragged away by some stranger. She had to do something. She couldn't let go of it. She was downright weary and looked the part. Dark circles were forming under her eyes. As tired as she was, she couldn't bear the thought of another torturous night of tossing and turning.

She pulled the clip from her hair and poured herself a cup of coffee. "I'm calling the police," she said bluntly, never looking up. I've given this a lot of thought and I'm reporting this business about Con Gordy."

"And tell them what? There ain't no evidence that she ever saw anybody," Andy said, emphasizing each word. "We ain't got nothin' to go on." He took a sip of his coffee. "And who's gonna take the word of a young'un anyway?"

Lisa didn't answer. She grabbed the phone and dialed 911.

"Lisa, put the phone down! It's ten o'clock at night. They're gonna think we're a bunch of lunatics."

She ignored him. The phone was answered on the first ring.

"Sheriff's Office … Dispatch. Is this an emergency?" a mechanical-sounding voice inquired.

"No, I mean, yes. What I'm trying to say is that a strange man has been coming around talking to my four-year-old daughter. It's happened more than once. I'm really worried that someone is trying to kidnap her. A few days ago he appeared at our front door. My daughter opened the door and he talked to her for a few minutes. By the time I got there he was gone." Lisa knew this sounded strange. A while back he showed up in our back yard, fenced back yard I might add, and told her he wanted to be her friend.

"Where is your daughter now ma'am?" He cleared his throat.

"She's in bed."

"Do you feel threatened right now?"

"No. Not right now."

"Give me your name and address. We'll have an officer come out and get a full report.

Andy had been cleaning his gun earlier that evening but thought he'd better put it away—probably not a good idea to have it out when the police arrived.

Forty-five minutes later a patrol car pulled into the driveway, the alarm silent, lights flashing. A young, uniformed officer exited the patrol car and pulled out a high-beam spotlight. He began making passes through trees and shrubs—the powerful light taking in areas in and around the back yard. He did not approach the house until he was satisfied no trespasser was hidden on the Wyrick premises.

He wrote a report based on the facts Lisa and Andy gave him. His manner was very professional, pausing occasionally, raising one eyebrow and staring at them intently. If he thought this a strange story, he didn't voice it; however, his body language told a whole different story.

"One more thing before I go." He stood up and took his pen out of his pocket. "Did either one of *you* actually *see* this man?"

"No, we didn't," Andy said, "but we believe our daughter's tellin' the truth."

"We'll have a car patrol this neighborhood for the next few days. We'll let you know if anything turns up."

"Thank you for coming," Lisa said. She closed the door, deadbolted the lock and leaned her back up against it. She heard the car as it backed out the drive. Just sharing the burden seemed to lift some of its weight from her shoulders.

"You really think she just made it all up, don't you? You know, like an imaginary friend?"

Andy didn't answer.

Lisa walked over and plopped down next to him on the sofa. "I know you say you believe her, but I get the funny feeling you really don't."

"What makes you think that? I do believe her, but the whole thing's weird for the fact that nobody around here can shed any light on it, Lisa. We can't prove a thing. Nothin's turned up in all these months. Nothin'." Andy rubbed his nose with his thumb and adjusted his ball cap. "First she sees a man dressed to the hilt in a black suit. Now she's sayin' that somebody, with God only knows what kind'a injury to his arm, shows up at the front door with blood all over'im."

"Well she'd have to have a pretty good imagination to come up with these stories." She was aggravated and it showed. She didn't care. Her nerves were stretched tight, like a rubber band about to snap, and she needed to release some tension. "Pick up those coffee cups and put them in the kitchen sink. I'll wash 'em tomorrow." Her tone was demanding.

Lisa didn't get mad often but, when she did, you didn't mess with her. Andy had learned when to argue and when not to, and this definitely wasn't the time.

He started toward the kitchen with the coffee cups, murmuring under his breath about having to pick up the dishes. He was stopped mid-stride at the kitchen door by the sight of the dog crouched near the kitchen table. He was snarling, his lips curled up exposing long, sharp fangs, his attention directed at some unseen threat. Wolf backed away slowly, his yellow eyes never leaving the kitchen.

"What is it boy?" Andy placed a comforting hand on Wolf's head, but the dog kept growling. Something had spooked him. *That's strange*, Andy thought. He'd never seen Wolf act like that. Andy felt a sudden adrenalin rush and gathering his courage, stepped into the kitchen. It was empty. A sudden chill passed over him. His heartbeat became erratic and he could feel a tingling up and down his spine. Suddenly he felt like a stranger in his own home and every instinct told him someone was in that room, watching. He couldn't see a presence, but he felt it.

11

THE REVELATION

In June of 1990, the house next door to Lisa came on the market and her sister Joyce, with advice from her parents, quickly signed a contract. She was newly divorced and raising two teenagers on her own. They thought it was a great buy and she would be close to her sister. Lisa was seventeen years her junior, not much older than her own children, but they'd always been close.

The house sat on a square, one-acre lot. Joyce had prayed many times for just one little acre and this was her answer. She knew the history of the old home place from Lisa's neighbor. She'd learned that the property had been owned by her family since 1914 and that it had been passed down through three generations. The old plank home had been torn down ten years earlier and replaced with a mobile home. The land, though, remained unchanged. Pecan trees, wild honeysuckle and magnolias had graced these grounds for many years. The old well was still usable.

The house immediately felt like home to Joyce and her children—Richard was nineteen years old and Niki, her daughter, had just turned sixteen. Since the children were older and stayed busy with friends, Joyce spent too much time alone. So, living next door to her sister was the perfect antidote.

After two months in the new house, things were finally shaping up. Richard had hauled off the last of the boxes a few days ago and the house was finally organized. On Saturday morning Joyce could finally relax out on the deck with her cup of coffee. She had been raised in the country and had always wanted to move back. Out here you could smell the honeysuckle, hear the birds chirping. It was almost hypnotizing. She breathed in deeply, giving a long sigh as she felt tension leave her body.

Lazily observing her landscaping, one majestic pecan tree seemed to stand out. It was mesmerizing—maybe because of its massive size and age, or maybe because it was so full of character. As she looked up into its enormous, moss-covered branches she felt there was something special about it. *If trees could talk,* she thought, *this one could tell many interesting stories.* She was sure it had seen many children playing under it, climbing up high in its branches—old men and women who kept cool under its shade on hot summer days. An old swing hung from a high limb, you could hear it creaking as it gently swayed back and forth in the wind.

Later that morning Joyce received a phone call from the previous owner. She called to ask if she could come by and drop off some old papers she'd come across while unpacking her belongings—papers that pertained to the property. She thought at some point they may be of use.

She arrived promptly at ten as she'd promised and was tickled to see the old home place. She walked nostalgically through the house and then the yard, wistfully stopping to smell honeysuckle that was just beginning to bloom—bending over to pick up a piece of roofing shingle from the old house that was still embedded in the grass. It had been hard to leave, she told Joyce. She'd practically lived there her whole life and had many childhood memories.

Seated in the living room talking, Joyce absently picked up the documents she had brought, her eyes quickly scanning the pages. A tri-folded warranty deed was tucked away in a long narrow envelope that was brittle and brown with age. Joyce pulled it out and carefully unfolded the thick paper. Glancing at the bottom she saw a name that made her blood run cold. She couldn't believe what she read. It was a revelation she didn't expect. It had been signed years ago by a man named Gordy!

It was moments before she could speak without her voice trembling but she questioned the former owner about the name. The woman had been a child then, she said, but remembered Mr. Gordy. She recalled that he loved children and that he was always dressed in a black suit and a top hat. It seemed as though he was sort of a grandfather figure, but that had been a long time ago. She said he had been dead more than thirty years.

It was hard for Joyce to keep her composure as she watched the car pull out of the drive and onto the two-lane road in front of the house. What she'd learned would change the course of events and answer some long-awaited questions. She had to tell her sister.

Joyce felt both agitated and excited as she pushed open Lisa's back door. "Lisa, I know who Mr. Gordy is!" She could hardly contain the news.

Lisa stopped dead in her tracks, twisting around to stare at her sister. "What!"

"Yep. You heard me right." Joyce's voice cracked. It was somewhere between crying and laughter. "Come read it for yourself, Lisa." She tossed the document on the kitchen table and smoothed it out flat, pointing out the name at the bottom.

Lisa looked at her sister, a petite brunette; hair twisted and pulled up with clip, hazel eyes; a legacy of maternal ancestors. She sat at the kitchen table staring at Lisa, the depths of her eyes portraying excitement, awe and fear—two sisters communicating without words. There was a keen awareness that neither realized they possessed; a phenomenon that sometimes exists between siblings or between mother and child.

Lisa sat the bowl she was holding on the counter and moved toward the table in the fashion of an old woman, as if she had an albatross hanging around her neck weighing her down. She dropped into a chair and picked up the Warranty Deed with her index finger and thumb as though it was a coiled snake. She began scanning it until her eyes rested on the signature at the bottom of the page. She read aloud, pronouncing each syllable slowly, "William S. Gordy." And, as if she didn't believe her own eyes, she read it again and again.

"Surely you don't think this is Heidi's Mr. Gordy," knowing deep down that it very well could be.

"I don't believe in coincidences Lisa. Look at the facts. Heidi has been seeing and talking to a person she calls Mr. Gordy for a long time. Then the name shows up on the Warranty Deed to the property next door and it's a good possibility that he owned the very land you live on. I asked questions when the deed was dropped off. Guess what, the man has been dead for thirty years! *Thirty years,* Lisa. She knew him ... knew his habits, what kind of clothes he wore, and whether we like it or not, it fits with everything Heidi's told us!"

"But what about the name Con? Where does that fit in?"

"I don't know. But I do believe this solves part of the puzzle."

Lisa put her head in her hands and wept.

"It never was a kidnapper, was it? It's the spirit of a dead man that visits her. That's why we've never seen him. That's the creepiest thing I've ever heard." Lisa felt as limp as a dish rag.

"Well, so far, it hasn't seemed to upset Heidi and that's a good thing."

"I guess you're right." Lisa was dabbing at her eyes. "But this doesn't make things any easier."

"And besides that, remember when you were Heidi's age, you saw things. In fact I remember you seeing a man similar to the man Heidi sees."

"Yes, but the difference is I never carried on conversations with him. I never was his 'friend.' He never told me his name!" she cried. "Whatever it is, we've got to put a stop to it, Joyce. You've got to help me."

"Well two things are for sure, you can't live with it and you can't kill it. If it's spiritual, the only viable weapon we've got is prayer. The Bible says when two are in agreement … it *will* be done. So let's agree that we bind it from this house in Jesus' name.

Each lay a hand down on the table, one on top of the other. They both agreed.

Thunder akin to a sonic boom split the night—rain pelting her arms like a spray of needles as Joyce sprinted through the wet grass toward home. It was late but she'd waited for Andy, not wanting to leave her sister alone with the blow she'd just been dealt.

As she reached the steps she felt compelled to turn, catching a glimpse of something black out of the corner of her eye as it darted across a lighted window—or was the stinging rain that hit her face and eyes with a vengeance causing illusions? Fear struck her as she ran for the safety of her own home.

12

SEARCHING FOR CLUES

Andy walked down the hallway with Lisa on his heels. He stood for a long moment, watching Heidi as she played, trying to absorb the news Lisa had just sprung on him. He felt Lisa's warm breath on his neck as she laid her head against him. This was one time he *hoped* his wife was exaggerating. A living, breathing human being could be hunted down and dealt with. A man's job was to protect his family, but how could you protect anyone from something you couldn't see; a being that can step in or out of an existence beyond the visible universe. There didn't seem to be an answer. He'd done all he could physically do but now he felt like this was a spiritual battle. He couldn't go it alone.

They lay in bed that night, held captive by their own thoughts. Finally, after all these months, something had materialized.

Lisa decided that she would immediately begin searching for clues to connect Heidi's stories of Mr. Gordy to the man who had signed the warranty deed on her sister's house. Morning couldn't come soon enough. She was anxious to get started.

What Lisa didn't know about detective work, she soon found out. She and her sisters started an exhaustive search beginning with local cemeteries. Days turned into weeks as they delved into huge mounds of paperwork, combing phone books, asking questions, trying to find any clue that would enlighten them. This was something they had to do for Heidi, for her protection and for the sanity of the entire family.

Each morning Lisa would drop Heidi off at school and continue investigating with either Joyce or another sister, Ester. Ester is your typical fiery redhead, hot tempered and determined—the perfect person to help Lisa in her search for factual information about Mr. Gordy.

The girls trampled though graveyards looking for the Gordy family name without success. The phone book yielded nothing. Only five Gordy names were listed and phone calls verified no connection to the warranty deed signature. They searched newspaper obituaries and death notice archives beginning more than thirty years earlier—but still no connection.

Lisa would never give up, would never allow fear to control their lives. Fear was a dangerous entity. If fear was left to run ramped it could actually kill. No, there was no place in their home for that kind of spirit no matter how long it took her to get to the bottom of things. And she wasn't alone—her family was behind her one hundred percent. The strong family bonds gave her the strength and the courage to continue looking. They were all desperate for answers.

Lisa looked at her watch. It was one-thirty. They had been at the library most of the day searching archives. "We've gotta go soon, Ester. Heidi'll be out of school in an hour and I don't want her waiting outside by herself."

Ester stood up and stretched, "I'm ready when ..."

"Here it is. I found him!" Lisa shouted.

"Where?"

"Here, look." Lisa pointed to the death notice.

"It is him." Esther read aloud, "Williams S. Gordy, born, 1898, died 1972. Services to be held at Magnolia Hill Cemetery. No wonder we couldn't find his grave. He wasn't even buried in this county."

So, Mr. Gordy had really lived and walked the property that Joyce now owned. They were both elated and terrified by the evidence they had uncovered.

The next week they began to search warranty deeds and tax records at the county courthouse. It seemed like weeks that they searched the dusty, thick books, volume after volume. Since his name showed up on the warranty deed to Joyce's property, they wanted to see what other properties he had owned. They finally hit pay dirt! They found not just one listing, but several. In fact, Mr. Gordy had once owned most of the land on Swint Loop, including Lisa and Andy's.

Ester looked at Joyce. "Let's go to your house for a cup of coffee. I think we deserve it."

"Do you have time Lisa?" Joyce said.

"Yeah, sure. I'll pick up Heidi and come on." She was worn out and desperately needed a break." That would be nice."

So the camaraderie continued at Joyce's kitchen table. Simmering down after awhile, each sister was consumed with her own thoughts.

They could tie Mr. Gordy to Lisa's property through courthouse records—they also knew he'd been dead for thirty years. What they didn't know was why he was here now and what it would take to get him to leave.

They had created a paradox: on one hand they knew everything; on the other hand they knew nothing!

"What next?" Lisa asked.

Three pairs of familial eyes stared at each other intently, each waiting for an answer from the others. None was forthcoming. Not yet.

13

SMOTHERED

Saturday morning dawned hot and humid and there wasn't a cloud in the sky. It was August and going to be a scorcher. Lisa had a list of chores for Andy—mowing the lawn was at the top of the list.

Heidi was ensconced on the sofa watching Saturday morning cartoons. Lisa heard childish laughter coming from the living room and she smiled to herself. It was good to hear Heidi laugh. It felt good to enjoy a semblance of a normal family. The last few months had been quiet. There had been no accounts from Heidi about strange visitors. Life appeared to be settling down—getting back to normal. They'd take this opportunity to get some things done outside. Besides, her parents were coming for dinner and she wanted to spruce up the front lawn. She grabbed her work gloves and headed out the front door.

Heidi became subconsciously aware of danger, moments before her brain sent the signal. A shadow came over her. She turned and saw him. Intuition made her want to jump up and run, but panic kept her rooted to the chair. Terror flooded her little body, causing her heart to beat dangerously fast. As she opened her mouth to cry out, the pillow came down over her face. She kicked and screamed but her cries were muffled. She struggled with all her might, trying hard to push away the heavy feather pillow—she couldn't breathe. Her arms and legs felt too heavy to lift. She felt as if she was floating. Then the pillow was gone and she gasped for air. She finally mustered up enough strength to scream—and scream she did. She screamed to the top of her lungs.

Andy reached the end of the yard, turned the mower, and began cutting another row. He stopped briefly to wipe his forehead. He was almost finished, thank God. He hated mowing grass. He was going fishing this afternoon and he was making a mental list of what he needed to pick up at the bait and tackle store. He was pulled from his thoughts when he saw Lisa running toward the house. She was gesturing frantically for him to come, calling out something he couldn't hear. He quickly switched off the lawnmower engine.

"What is it?" he yelled.

"It's Heidi. Hurry! She must be hurt."

Andy nearly tripped over the gas can he'd left sitting in the yard as he bolted toward the house. He was on Lisa's heels as they scrambled to get to the front door. Heidi lay crumpled in the corner of the couch with her blanket pulled around her chin, her eyes wide with fear. Hot tears streamed down her red, sweaty face; damp strings of long, dark hair clung to her forehead.

"What's the matter?"

"That man ... that man put a pillow over my face," she sobbed. "I couldn't breath. I'm scared. Make him go away! Make him leave me alone!"

Andy ran for the back door. Although he hadn't seen anyone enter the house, he couldn't be sure no one had. It was Saturday and they hadn't left home all day. The back door was locked and the front door had been in plain sight while they were in the yard. The only way anyone could enter was through a window, but they were locked and nailed shut. Andy made sure the house was secure after Heidi's first encounter with Mr. Gordy.

He frantically searched every square inch of the house anyway, just to be sure, but there was no sign of an intruder. He hurried out the front door and around the house. He looked up and down the road but saw no one.

He could feel his heart pounding as he hurried back inside, taking Heidi from Lisa's arms. He held her tightly and whispered, "I checked the whole house and there's nobody here, Heidi. Shhhhh … It's okay now. You must'a had a bad dream."

Heidi sniffed and wiped her eyes "But it wasn't a dream, Daddy. It was real. The man put the pillow over my head. I couldn't breathe."

Questioning her at this point would be futile, Lisa thought. Right now, calming her fears was the most important thing. "Don't cry, honey, everything will be alright." Lisa sat beside them, stroking Heidi's long, dark hair.

"I don't like that man, Momma. I couldn't see his face." She sobbed hysterically for what seemed like hours. She clung desperately to her mother—unable to be comforted.

Fear is not part of the human makeup at birth. Fear is a learned emotion stemming from the anticipation of danger. Heidi was never afraid of Mr. Gordy or Con, probably because she didn't sense a threat. Now she had been introduced not only to fear but caution and distrust.

14

THE SCRATCHES

The sound of Heidi crying quickly jolted Lisa awake. Memories of the pillow incident a week ago were still fresh in her mind. As her eyes adjusted, she could see Heidi standing there holding one side of her face. She glanced at the clock and saw that it was four-thirty.

"What is it, Heidi? Did you have a bad dream?" Lisa rubbed her eyes.

"No, Momma. My face hurts."

"Come here, honey." Lisa said, pulling her daughter close. She stretched her arm across the table and turned on the bedside lamp. "Let me see." She gently pried Heidi's hand away from her face and turned it toward the light. Three long scratches resembling claw marks marred Heidi's smooth skin. The scratches went deep and blood oozed from her cheek, just below her right eye.

"Andy, wake up!" Lisa shouted. Andy was a heavy sleeper.

"Andy, wake up and look at Heidi's face!"

"What's the matter?" He rolled over, holding one hand up to shield his eyes from the light.

"Look at Heidi's face. It's bleeding! Look at these awful scratches!" Lisa turned Heidi's cheek so Andy could see.

One look at his daughter was enough to quickly roust Andy. "What in the world happened to her?"

"I don't know," Lisa said.

Andy swung his legs over the side of the bed, grabbed his jeans from the chair and slid into them as fast as he could. A quick search of the house revealed nothing out of the ordinary.

Lisa took Heidi to the bathroom, sat her on top of the counter and gently cleaned the wounds. She found it difficult to keep her composure. She was afraid of what she didn't know and what she didn't understand.

Bewildered and frightened, they all three huddled together in bed, Heidi in the middle. In the safety of her parent's bed Heidi soon drifted off to sleep, but, unable to rest, Lisa and Andy lay awake until daylight.

They both looked haggard, eyes swollen from lack of sleep as they sat drinking coffee the next morning. They hashed and rehashed recent events, neither able to come up with answers or suggest a plan of action. So many strange things had happened since they moved into the house.

As they talked, Lisa told Andy about an incident that happened a while back. It was something that had totally escaped her mind until just now. Heidi couldn't have been much more than two-and-a-half years old at the time.

They had been shopping and decided to stop by Joyce's to visit. During the visit, Lisa decided she needed her hair trimmed and Joyce gladly obliged. As they sat and talked at the vanity, Heidi wandered into the walk-in closet. There wasn't anything in there that could hurt her so they didn't pay it much attention. The sisters talked about this and that and for a while, then began to wonder what Heidi was doing.

After a few minutes Lisa got up to check on her. "What are you doing in there, honey?" she asked.

"Talking to a lady," Heidi replied.

"What lady?" Joyce asked puzzled.

"That lady," Heidi replied.

"What did she say?"

"Nothing. She's dead."

That was creepy, very creepy coming from a two-year-old. Looking back on that incident, Lisa wondered if that was the beginning of this whole nightmare—that was until she remembered the strange black woman the day Heidi was born.

"I feel like I'm goin' crazy, Lisa," Andy told her as he poured more coffee.

"Well, don't think you own the patent on crazy, Andy. If we had good insurance I'd be getting psychiatric help right now. I'm totally overwhelmed. I don't know what to think or what to do. I hate living with this constant anxiety."

"Well, all I know is we can't go on like this. Either we figure out what's goin' on in the house, or we've gotta get out—find somewhere else to go. I gotta feelin' we ain't safe here."

Andy was right, they weren't safe. A week later he awoke to an intense, burning pain on his back. Jumping out of bed he shook Lisa awake."

"Lisa, get up and look at my back. It feels like it's on fire." He was pulling off his shirt as fast as he could.

"My God, Andy, you've got deep scratches down your back just like Heidi had, only these are deeper and longer."

Andy was terror stricken as he examined his back and sides in the bathroom mirror. Whatever attacked him had drawn blood.

Andy was in a tizzy. He wanted to get in his truck and leave. He wanted to sell the house.

Eventually Lisa calmed him down. She cleaned and bandaged his wounds.

They talked until after midnight but could come up with no plan. They couldn't afford to sell the house. None of the family had room for them.

"I'm scared Lisa," Andy said, "and I ain't never been scared of nothin'. You know I ain't. If I could see it, I'd kill it or die tryin'."

It didn't seem as though they had any options. For now Heidi would have to sleep with them. She was their main concern. Of all the times they'd calmed their screaming, frightened daughter, she'd never been physically hurt until now. Something would have to give.

15

THE DARK FIGURE

Four-and-a-half years had passed since they'd moved into the house on Swint Loop and paranormal manifestations continued. Nothing had come of the fact that Mr. Gordy's name was found on courthouse records, but he continued to make himself known only to Heidi. She remained adamant that there was no discernible difference between Mr. Gordy and anyone else. *He looks just like me or you,* she said more than once. A constant feeling of mental unrest weighed heavily on Lisa and Andy.

It was 1993. Lisa had suffered two miscarriages the previous year, but was now pregnant and in her second trimester. Her belly was beginning to protrude like a giant watermelon.

The baby was a girl. Lisa was hoping that with a new sister, Heidi's attention would be diverted from Mr. Gordy.

"Heidi, come quick!" Lisa yelled.

Heidi dropped a couple of books into a storage box and hustled down the hall to see what her mother wanted. It sounded urgent.

Lisa had just stepped out of the shower and was standing in front of the mirror with a towel draped around her, her hair still dripping wet.

"Put your hand right here." Lisa took Heidi's small hand and guided it to her protruding belly and placed it flatly against her skin.

"Do you feel that?"

"Yeah, but what is it?"

"That's the baby's foot. She's kicking up a storm today." They looked at each other and smiled.

"I'll be so glad when she gets here. I'm picking out some of my books to give her." Heidi paused. "How much longer will it be anyhow?"

"About four months, but I think she's getting a little impatient. I think she wants to get out and play with her big sister."

Heidi laughed delightedly. "I've thought of a good name for her."

"Oh, yeah?" Lisa said. She reached over and adjusted the sleeve of Heidi's shirt.

"I want to name her Jordan."

"Where'd that name come from," Lisa was brushing her hair.

"One of my books. She's a girl who dresses in bright colors. She makes her hair stick up all over her head and does crazy things. She tries to cover up her feelings that no one likes or understands her. I like her. I like her name, too."

"Let's get the baby book and see what it means."

Lisa kept the book handy because they hadn't settled on a name yet. They sat side by side on the couch as Lisa thumbed through it looking for the Js.

"Here it is." Lisa began to read.

Jordan. This Hebrew name is that of the Jordan River and means 'flowing downward.' John the Baptist baptized Jesus Christ in its waters and it was adopted as a personal name after crusaders brought back water from the river to baptize their children.

"Well, I like it too," Lisa smiled, "but I still need to see what your daddy thinks."

"He'll like it."

"Have you put your books away?"

"I'm almost done. I'm giving my sister, *"Have You Seen my Mother,"* since that was my favorite book when I was little. And I'm giving her my Dr. Seuss books, too.

Lisa was smiling as she picked up the Harris County Journal and lay back on the couch. She tired easily these days.

Heidi sat on the floor in her room going through her books, putting some aside for the baby and straightening the rest. She began to feel the odd sense that someone was there and glanced around candidly.

"Mr. Gordy, is that you?"

Her eyes fell on a cloaked, dark figure standing just inside her closet—unseen eyes hidden by the hood he wore as he watched her. She could physically feel the evil that it oozed into the room.

Lisa was reading the headlines when she heard Heidi's screams. Before she could get up, Heidi burst into the room. Tears were streaming down her face.

Lisa leapt to her feet, panicked. She thought Heidi was hurt.

"What is it?"

"There's a man in my room!" she screamed. "He's in my closet!"

Lisa didn't know what to do. She grabbed Heidi's hand, snatched up the cordless phone and headed for the back door. Upset, she dialed Joyce's phone number.

"Joyce, Heidi just saw a man in her room! Get down here, quick, and bring the gun!" Lisa was almost whispering.

"Where are you now?"

"We're standing in the kitchen by the back door. Hurry."

"I'm on the way." Joyce burst through the back door in seconds with her revolver in hand.

"He's in there. He's in there!" Heidi said as she clutched her aunt's arm.

They all three crept slowly down the hallway and into Heidi's room. The door to the closet was open slightly. They stood there for a moment, scared to open it. After finally building up a little courage, Joyce pushed the door open wider. They all three stood there, gazing into an empty closet. Relief was intense.

"See there, Heidi. Nobody's in here," Joyce said.

"He *was* in there," Heidi insisted.

"Did you get a good look at him?" Joyce asked.

"No. He wouldn't ... let ... me see his ... face. That's why I was ... so scared."

"Calm down, Heidi. Everything's okay."

"He was something dark and scary—his face was hidden. That's all I saw." She clung to her mother's arm.

"Was it Mr. Gordy?" Lisa asked.

"No!" Heidi cried. "It was somebody else—somebody bad."

Let's go to my house until this settles down," Joyce suggested. Lisa agreed.

The following months brought chaos to the Wyrick family. Inexplicable phenomena became a daily occurrence. Things disappeared and reappeared for no apparent reason. Lisa would find cabinet doors standing open in the kitchen at odd hours of the day. The kitchen faucets would turn on full blast. One day while her niece was there, a chair actually moved from under the dining room table and twirled around facing the living room where they sat. It was the kind of behavior that make most people think Poltergeists, but Lisa believed she was just being toyed with, and that made her very nervous.

Andy was nervous too. "I sleep every night with one eye closed and one eye lookin' down the hallway," he told his father-in-law one evening when they were visiting. "If I ever see *anything*, I'm leavin' and I ain't comin' back. I'm goin' with or without the rest of the family!"

The *dark figure*, as Heidi began calling the entity, started manifesting itself with greater frequency and with more intensity. From what Lisa could determine, Heidi's description was that of a dark shadow with a human outline. It had no facial features. It was vindictive and evil and seemed to wish harm on their family. Why? What in the world had they done to deserve this?

16

BURIED TREASURE

Summer seemed to come and go quickly, and in September, Heidi began second grade. Academically she was functioning at a much higher level than most of her peers and excelled in all her subjects—especially art and music. She looked forward to school. She enjoyed riding the bus and quickly became friends with Montein, who sat directly across the aisle in her assigned seat. They were the same age and Heidi found it easy to talk to her. Montein was her best friend now, with the exception of Mr. Gordy.

Joyce followed bus number twenty-eight as it bounced down Swint Loop. She could see two boys in the back with their heads bobbing up and down, their rear ends being jolted clear off the seat as the bus hit every pothole in the road. The bus came to a halt making all kinds of racket—gears grinding, brakes squealing. As she got closer to the house she could see Lisa standing outside waiting for Heidi. Joyce pulled into her driveway, stopping briefly to speak to Lisa.

The bus doors opened and Heidi bounded down the steps. She was a bundle of energy.

"Hey Aunt Joyce," Heidi called out.

She looked at her mother. "Momma, can I go to Aunt Joyce's house, please?"

"I'm sure you have homework to do, Heidi."

"But it's really important," she pleaded. "Please, can I go?"

Concealing a smile, Joyce met Lisa's eyes, both wondering what was so vital.

"Go on, if Aunt Joyce don't care. But you need to get your homework done before supper. It's church night."

"Oh Lisa, you know I don't care, "Joyce said. "I picked up a new sketchpad for her today anyway. I was going to bring it over later."

Heidi handed her book bag to her momma and started up the hill.

Joyce pulled up a little further and shoved the car in park. Heidi looked radiant today, her long dark hair bouncing as she climbed the hill. Today she had on a deep blue dress that accentuated her striking eyes. Yellow, embroidered daisies stood out along the hemline.

They strolled across the yard and onto the back deck. Joyce unlocked the door and they stepped into the kitchen.

"Boy, I can't wait to hear the important news." Joyce kicked off her shoes and threw her purse onto the kitchen counter.

"Mr. Gordy wants you to know a secret." Heidi explored the counter looking for the cookie jar.

"What? What are you talking about Heidi?"

"He wants me to tell you something." She reached in the jar and snagged a couple of chocolate chip cookies.

Joyce was astonished at the casual way Heidi was acting. It was as if this was no big deal. "Mr. Gordy knows *me*?" She swallowed hard, a huge lump in her throat. She didn't wait for an answer. "What'd he say?"

"He said to tell you there's money buried in your yard."

"*What?*" Joyce took in a deep breath. "Did he say *where*?" she managed to ask.

"Yeah. Come on and I'll show you." Heidi grabbed Joyce's hand leading her to the back yard. "It's right over here by the tree." She pointed to a patch of ground near the base of the large old pecan tree near the swing.

Joyce stepped carefully, her bare feet tender as she stepped among the broken pecan shells. The swing hung limp from one of the lower branches of the tree. The rope was twisted and gnarled, the old wooden seat cracked and weathered from years of wear.

So that's it! She thought. *From the day I moved in I knew there was something about that old tree.* Sometimes when the wind stirred though the leaves you'd swear you heard laughter.

Joyce borrowed a metal detector from her brother, Marcus, and over the next few weeks she, Lisa and Heidi scanned the area around the base of the old tree. The equipment was not of professional quality and could only pick up metals in shallow ground. All they found were drink tabs and other metal pieces of no value.

It was more than possible that there was buried treasure around here. During the Civil War, many people hid money, silver, jewelry and who knows what else, in the ground to keep the Yankees and pillagers from taking it. *But if there is money buried here*, Joyce thought, *it's probably Confederate and of little or no value.*

Eventually they gave up the search. They had no help, no equipment and not enough strength to dig very deep in the red Georgia clay. Someday, when they had better equipment, they might try again.

17

Silk Ribbons

Months passed and Heidi still talked of Mr. Gordy and sometimes about Con. There had been no recent visits, though, from the intimidating dark figure. Thank God for that. Hopefully this phase of Heidi's life had passed.

In February 1994, Lisa gave birth to a beautiful baby girl. They named her Jordan. Although Andy had hoped for a boy, his new daughter was a total delight to him—a robust healthy child with a head full of dark brown, curly hair. Jordan brought new joy to the Wyrick home. Heidi was especially enthralled with her baby sister. But the serenity the Wyrick's felt before Jordan was born was short lived.

Niki, Joyce's daughter, was sitting with Jordan while Lisa took Heidi to school. She had errands to run in town and wouldn't be back until lunch, and Andy had left before daylight. Niki enjoyed watching Jordan and since her first baby would be here soon, it would give her much needed practice.

The house felt cold. Jordan finished her bottle and was asleep in Niki's arms in no time. The fire in the wood-burning heater had died down and needed more fuel. She decided to put Jordan in her crib and put another log on the fire. It was still early.

Niki felt a cold draft in the room. She laid the baby in her crib, tucked the blanket snugly around her, then checked the window above the bed. It was shut tight. She ran her hand along the window sill but didn't feel any air coming through. *That's odd*, she thought, *I wonder where that cold wind is coming from.* She grabbed Lisa's robe off the rocking chair and slung it around her shoulders, then went to the kitchen to start a pot of coffee.

March winds blew hard and she heard the windows rattle as she placed three small logs in the wood heater. The heat was warm on her face as she watched the flames flickering through the iron grate. The fire was mesmerizing. She heard the coffee pot beep and the aroma drew her to the kitchen. A cup of brew in hand, Niki pulled the throw up around her neck and downed the hot coffee with fervor. She slid into a comfortable position on the sofa and quickly succumbed to its warmth.

She was at work—but then again she wasn't. The desk was strewn with dozens of charts—she didn't recognize a single name. Strange. She couldn't remember what she was supposed to do. Her nerve endings were tingling.

"Nik keeeeeee," no louder than a whisper

She looked up not sure she heard anything.

"Nik … keeeeee," louder now.

"I'm in here, who is it?"

No answer.

She rose from the desk backing up against the wall. Something wasn't right. She hadn't seen another soul and the quiet was deafening. Uneasiness assailed her.

Her eyes took in the long rectangular room. The walls were a cold, steel color and the floors were made of concrete. There were no windows. Along one wall were four-drawer file cabinets—maybe twenty, maybe more. She had no idea if it was day or night, the only illumination being a single cord hanging from the ceiling with a bare bulb. Where was everybody?

A loud metallic sound abruptly broke the silence, followed by the sound of running water. She stood rooted to the spot for what seemed an eternity. Turning her head to scan the room once again she noticed a steel door with a panic bar. She was certain it hadn't been there before. Her heart was hammering, resounding in her own ears.

A whimpering noise suddenly split the silence. What was that? At first she thought it sounded like a wounded animal. If that was the case she'd need to help it, wouldn't she? She edged toward the steel door, easing it open, passing through it before she lost nerve. Nobody was in there, so where'd the sounds come from? She looked around. A long steel table ran almost the length of the room—irrigated canals ran along both sides. As her eyes moved around the room, the horror of her situation assaulted her and it was chilling. This was a morgue. She heard the whimper again. She ran, slamming the steel door behind her, her nervous fingers trying to find a lock. There wasn't one. She could hear her own labored breathing—hear the beat of her heart as it seemed to reverberate off the steel walls.

She somehow felt impelled to put up the charts. Her legs felt weighted down as she began moving toward the desk. Grabbing several, she quickly walked to the file cabinet. Opening the drawer, she stared incoherently inside, falling to her knees—her hand on the file drawer the only thing holding her up. Minutes went by before she pulled herself back up and peered through watery eyes at a dead infant, laid out as if in a pathetic little grave. Panic stricken she opened the next drawer and the next drawer—this was a mausoleum! Oh, God. She opened her mouth to scream but no sound came. As her head nodded backward out of pity and deep compassion, she noticed the room had no ceiling. She was looking at the sky. As she watched, white clouds parted and a disembodied face appeared. Fierce eyes pulled her in and held her hostage as the lips began to move. No sound came from the entity—lips exaggerating each word, eyebrows furrowed—so great was the importance of the message.

Concentrating as hard as she could because she knew it was imperative, she still could not understand. Tears poured down her face. She'd failed to interpret the message that could mean life or death.

A sound broke into her dream—the sound of a baby whimpering. She jerked awake.

She looked at the clock. Her heart was pounding and beads of perspiration had popped out all over her face. The dream was unnerving. It was a little after eight. She'd put Jordan to bed only twenty minutes earlier. *She must be wet,* Niki thought. She tossed the throw onto the back of the sofa and went to check, unprepared for the scene she was about to witness.

"Oh my God!" she screamed.

Joyce was taking out the trash when she heard screams. It sounded like her daughter. She dropped the plastic trash bag and ran toward Lisa's house.

"Momma, help!"

It *was* Niki! She was running with a pink bundle in her arms. "Help!" She held Jordan's little body tightly in her left arm and her right hand was close to the baby's neck. She was hysterical and her hands were trembling.

Joyce met her half way across the yard. "What's the matter with her?" She threw the pink blanket back and gasped. A pink ribbon was tied tightly around Jordan's neck and her face was tinged with blue.

"Hurry, Momma. Get something to cut this off." Tears were streaming down Niki's face, her index finger held beneath the ribbon at the throat so Jordan could breathe.

"Get her in the house, quick!" Joyce bolted up the steps, Niki right behind her.

"Please hurry, momma. I don't know if she's breathing."

Joyce grabbed a small pair of cuticle scissors from the kitchen drawer and cut the ribbon. It had been tied in what seemed like hundreds of tiny knots.

"How in God's name did this happen!" She wasn't angry with Niki; she just needed an explanation. She needed to know who, or what for that matter, could have done such a cruel deed.

"I don't know. I heard her crying and when I went to check on her, I found the ribbon tied around her neck." Niki was crying, still trying to shake that horrible dream. "She'd only been in her crib about twenty minutes."

"Thank God she's alright." Joyce took Jordan and held her tightly against her bosom. "Shhhhh. Don't cry now."

"We need to check her out, Niki," Joyce said, as she laid the baby on the sofa and removed her clothes. Other than the ring around her neck made by the taut ribbon, she could find no other bruises or marks.

"Calm down Niki, she's gonna be fine, now. This is not your fault."

"I know Momma, but I shouldn't have left her in that room alone." Niki looked at Jordan and thought of the baby in her dream. It could have been her. Was this some sort of premonition or forewarning of something yet to come? If so, what was it? She had no answer.

"Did you see or hear anything before that, anything at all?"

"No. Nothing." She couldn't think straight right now. She was too shaken up. The dream was far too realistic. But for now, she thought it best not to mention the dream to her mother. Joyce was upset enough already.

It was eleven o'clock when Lisa returned home and she was completely beside herself when she learned of the morning's events, and even more shocked when she saw the marks that were still evident around Jordan's neck.

"I don't think I can take much more of this. We've heard things in the house for the past couple of nights but Andy says it's just the wind. I don't think so. Joyce, I'm scared, I'm really scared."

"I think your right. I believe something's in that house and it's not good."

Lisa immediately called her mother and asked her to be praying. Edna called her sister, Ruth, and they decided it would be best to come pray over Jordan's crib. Lisa was glad. Prayer always comforted her.

18

IDENTIFICATION OF A STRANGER

Silent intruders of the worst kind—the kind that bears ill will, the kind you can't see—entered and exited their home at will and there was nothing to be done about it. Lisa and Andy were crazy with worry. For an infant baby to actually be attacked proved they were all in horrible danger. Lisa, prone to migraine headaches, now had constant pain in her head and neck that even prescription drugs wouldn't help. She moved Jordan's crib into her bedroom and most of the time Heidi slept in their bed. The bad thing was she couldn't see an end to this nightmare. Who do you call?

She laid her book on the coffee table. She couldn't concentrate on anything right now. The incident with the silk ribbons had severely unnerved her. Her momma was a history buff and Lisa had borrowed a book from her on the Civil War. Lisa thought maybe, if she could actually locate the valuables that Mr. Gordy said was buried in Joyce's backyard, he'd leave Heidi alone. It was worth a shot. Momma said spirits visit you for a reason and when that reason has been put to rest, the spirit will rest, too.

Ellerslie, Georgia, was inhabited mostly by senior citizens as was certainly the case on Swint Loop. Elderly people love to talk as Lisa soon found out. Her next door neighbor's favorite topic was "the war," and she painted a vivid picture of what she remembered *"right here on this very land—Damn Yankees, that's what Poppa called'em. He always said, "a Yankee ain't worth the nuts off my most worthless mule."* She could go on for hours, sometimes coherently, sometimes not. But Lisa gained insight into events that happened a hundred and forty years ago on the land where they lived.

As she listened to the old folk a possible scenario began to form in her mind.

Marauders from Sherman's army rode south after burning Atlanta. As the war raged, people began burying money, jewelry and other items of value. It was highly possible that the little town of Ellerslie had been drenched with the blood of both Confederate and Union soldiers … maybe in an area behind Lisa's house, a hole was dug. Gold and other valuables were hastily put into a chamber pot and buried under the hog pen in a three-foot grave. Muck was shoveled over the broken earth. The old hog pen was now the north corner of the yard next door. "Oft' times as not," they'd said, "people were killed, died of disease or just moved on—valuables lost or forgotten, claimed by the earth."

"Momma, Mr. Gordy showed me where money is buried…"

The curtains billowed out, wind bringing in the scent of honeysuckle. Lisa drew in a long deep breath. At times she could believe everything was normal, that Heidi was just like every other kid in her class, but she knew deep down her child was different. She thought about Jordan. Would she have that same sensitivity? She prayed not.

"Momma, Mr. Gordy showed me where money is buried…"

She covered her ears with her hands as if to block out unwanted thoughts, her smoke colored hair falling around her hands and face. She laid back and closed her eyes, unable to prevent random thoughts from inundating her mind.

"Momma, why has Con got blood on his shirt?"

Heidi had correctly identified Con from a stack of old photographs Lisa borrowed from her former neighbor. She'd never forget that day. Heidi was sitting on the hearth—she and Joyce sitting cross-legged on the floor facing her. Neither of them really expected anything useful to come of it but the need to do anything at all was overwhelming.

"Look at these pictures Heidi," she'd said, "and see if you recognize anybody."

Heidi thumbed slowly through the pictures one by one, eventually focusing on a small snapshot lying on the bottom of the box. Old and faded, the black-and-white photo showed five men standing together. Heidi examined it closely.

"That's Con," Heidi said, without hesitation. She pointed to the man at the far left, his arms folded, one on top of the other.

Maybe we shouldn't discuss this in front of Heidi, Joyce thought. Her sister looked nervous.

"Heidi, maybe you should check on Wolf," Joyce said. "I noticed his water bowl was empty when I came up."

Heidi got up and ran out the back door, slamming it behind her.

Lisa looked at her sister. "That *is* him. That's Con. She's right, Joyce. He was my neighbor's uncle. According to her, he had a horrible accident at the cotton gin up the road and his hand got amputated. He'd stumbled home, arm wrapped in a piece of white cloth, blood everywhere. She said he was taken to the clinic for blood loss and shock. He's dead now."

Momma, why has Con got blood on his shirt? Lisa couldn't get Heidi's words out of her head.

"Good God," Joyce said, "I wish we'd never heard of Swint Loop." She shook her head vigorously. "How did you happen to get those pictures from that woman anyway?"

"I talked with her on the phone this morning and after I told her the story about Heidi seeing a man named Con, she became very interested. She said it sounded just like an uncle of hers who had passed on a long time ago. I ask her if she had pictures and she said she did. She brought them to me this morning and told me to keep them as long as I liked. I had no idea, I really didn't."

Joyce eventually had to go home, although she hated leaving Lisa by herself. Heidi and Jordan had gone to Andy's parents for the night and Andy's wasn't home yet. But Joyce had to work tomorrow and had a load of clothes to wash.

When Andy arrived home about eight o'clock, Lisa told him what happened with Con's picture. They were up most of the night talking about how to handle the whole situation and finally decided to call a parapsychologist at the University of Georgia. Lisa had tried before, but Andy wouldn't agree to it. She'd obtained the name and phone number for Dr. William Roll from the library a few weeks back. She would call him first thing in the morning.

Sleep eluded both Lisa and Andy, one scenario after another playing through their minds. They were anxious to talk with the doctor. The need for answers consumed them, making it impossible to rest.

19

THE PARAPSYCHOLOGIST

Heidi was mature for eight years old. She understood that she was different from most people. She knew she aroused curiosity and speculation. She felt distant from people, sometimes from her own family. She lay on her back on the trampoline looking up at the sky. She knew her family loved her, yet she sometimes felt completely alone in the world. She knew her mother understood—that's why she called this doctor. She wondered what he could do to help. Her mother had tried everything anyone suggested. So far there was no logical explanation for this *gift*, this *curse* she had been born with.

The sound of the phone ringing interrupted her thoughts. She could hear her mother talking. She got up and wandered closer to the door.

"Yes, this is Lisa." Lisa paused. "Oh hi, Dr. Roll, I've been expecting your call. Thanks for calling me back so quickly." She paused for a few moments. "Yes, that would be great. See you then."

Heidi didn't go in. She needed to be alone with her thoughts. She had mixed feelings about someone coming to talk to her, especially someone she didn't know. But if it made her mother feel better, she'd do it. She'd seen her mother cry enough, seen her daddy mad and upset. She would do whatever she could to make her parents happy.

The next afternoon Lisa stood watching anxiously out the window. At six-thirty. Dr. Roll arrived driving a blue Ford Taurus rental car. He walked up the driveway carrying a black bag.

Lisa stepped out onto the front porch and called out, "You must be Dr. Roll."

"Yes, that's right. And you must be Lisa." He spoke with a heavy British accent.

His openness and smile immediately put Lisa at ease. His appearance was that of a distinguished gentleman. He was dressed casually in creased pants and a long-sleeve shirt. His white hair was perfectly groomed although it touched his collar in the back.

He followed Lisa into the living room where Heidi sat on a blanket. She laid Jordan down next to Heidi and placed the activity swing over her. Jordan kicked and giggled at the sight of Elmo and his friends.

"Dr. Roll, this is Heidi." She motioned toward her oldest daughter. "And this is Jordan." Lisa reached down and rubbed Jordan's head in an attempt to tame the unruly curls.

He smiled, "Well, hello, Heidi. I'm so glad to finally meet you," Dr. Roll took her small hand in his. He behaved informally in a free-and-easy manner, making it apparent he'd worked with children in the past.

Heidi smiled at him shyly.

Andy appeared in the doorway. "This is my husband, Andy," Lisa said. Dr. Roll and Andy shook hands and exchanged greetings.

"Nice to meet you. Have a seat." Andy indicated the overstuffed chair in the living room.

"I'd rather sit 'round the table if we could," Dr. Roll suggested. "I'd like to get started as soon as possible." Everybody found a place to sit as Dr. Roll removed a small tape recorder, pen and notebook from his briefcase.

The session lasted about two hours. He'd prepared questions for Andy and Lisa as well as Heidi. "I'll have to admit I'm intrigued," he said, smiling broadly at Heidi.

He took his time questioning her. He didn't want to push her because sometimes children shut down if they feel backed into a corner. He was amazed at her lucid thinking. She was clear and consistent with her answers. He had prepared more than thirty questions and she answered every one. He'd only conversed with Lisa by telephone previously and was very interested in Heidi's story. After one session with her he was totally fascinated.

Over the next month, Dr. Roll visited twice. He'd accumulated mountains of information. The more he found out, the more interested he became.

Lisa and Andy kept wringing their hands in anticipation of Dr. Roll's findings.

The phone rang. It was Dr. Roll with what he described as good news. "I've located the Gordys," he said. "Luckily they have agreed to let me borrow a few family pictures. I received them in the mail yesterday. I'd like to bring them out and have Heidi examine them. I'm curious to see if she'll recognize anyone."

"Let me talk to Heidi and Andy and I'll call you right back," Lisa said.

"I'd like to bring my camera crew if it's alright. I'd like to get this on film."

"I don't see why not, but I'd like to make sure it's okay with the rest of the family. I'll call you back within the hour."

Heidi and Andy were both in the living room, Andy bouncing Jordan up and down on his knee, Heidi sorting out her box of pencils and markers." That was Dr. Roll on the phone, Heidi. He wants to bring over some pictures for you to look at. What do you think?"

"If that's what you want me to do," Heidi said.

"No, Heidi, it's up to you. If you don't want to look at the pictures I'll call Dr. Roll and tell him no."

"It's okay. I'll look at the pictures."

"Do you mind if he brings his camera?"

"I don't mind," Heidi said.

"What kind of pictures does he want her to look at?" Andy asked.

"I'll tell you later." Lisa dodged the question. "I have to call Dr. Roll back." It would be better if Heidi's opinion wasn't swayed in one way or the other.

Lisa called Joyce and told her what was going on. "Will you come over when he gets here?" she asked. She needed moral support. "Ask Niki if she'll watch Jordan. I'm afraid all the commotion will upset her."

Dr. Roll arrived for the appointment with a shoebox full of old photographs. He sat down at the table beside her and before opening the box he explained, "Heidi, I have some pictures here I'd like for you to look at, but before you do, I'd like to make sure you're okay with it."

Heidi agreed and Dr. Roll motioned for the camera man to set up his equipment. He instructed everyone in the room to be absolutely quiet.

When the cameraman nodded that he was ready, Dr. Roll began. "If anyone in the pictures looks familiar to you," he said, "I want you to put those aside." He was specific with his instructions. He opened the lid and took the photographs from the box, placing them on the table in front of her.

All eyes were upon her as she examined the pictures for the very first time—most of them decades older than she was. Tension was so thick in the room you could cut it with a knife. She picked up the pictures one at a time, examining them closely before laying them aside. The silence was deafening.

As she neared the bottom of the stack she picked up a five-by-seven photograph. Smiling broadly, she held it up. "This is my friend Mr. Gordy," she said.

His finger trembled as Dr. Roll pointed to the dingy photograph. "You're right, Heidi. That *is* Mr. Gordy," he assured her.

Lisa's eyes went from the old photograph to the roughly sketched portrait of a man Heidi had drawn. It was clear now that the sketch on her refrigerator, drawn by a much younger Heidi, was Mr. Gordy. The sketch was a little vague but Lisa saw the resemblance. She put her head down on the table and wept, streams of tears washing down her cheeks. She sobbed, not caring that the camera was still running.

Lisa hugged her daughter. "I'm sorry, Heidi."

"Its okay, Momma, please don't cry," she said, trying to console her mother as if their roles were reversed.

Heidi identified the only two pictures of Mr. Gordy in the stack of at least a hundred old photographs. She'd been right. There was a man named Mr. Gordy and another man named Con. None of it was imagination. She *had* seen them. She *had* talked with them. It was all true!

The identification of the two men was all that Heidi's parents needed to prove in their own minds what they'd suspected. Heidi possessed a special talent allowing her to see into another dimension. Heidi *could* communicate with the dead.

Dr. Roll was thrilled. "This is the first case I've studied where someone positively identified the spirits they claimed to have seen. "With your permission, I'd like to continue working with Heidi. I have some theories I'd like to discuss with the two of you, but I'll need a couple of weeks to write up my report."

"We'll have to think about it," Andy replied. "I've gotta give this some time to sink in."

"I understand. But, I have to tell you that this is the most interesting case I've ever worked with."

Lisa was still crying. She turned to Dr. Roll, "So, do you think this is something she'll outgrow?"

"To tell you the truth Lisa, I don't know. I've never had a case exactly like this."

Joyce chimed in, directing her statement to Dr. Roll. "She started seeing things when she was barely two years old. Now she's eight and she continues seeing things. Don't sound like she'll outgrow it to me."

"Maybe not." Dr. Roll stood up, picked up the stack of pictures and put them back inside the box. "I must be off, but if anything comes up, please call me. Meanwhile I'll be preparing my report."

He started toward the door and said his goodbyes. Lisa watched as he got back into his car and drove away.

The report came a few weeks later. Dr. Roll had examined several theories, but the one he felt the strongest about was that their house had been constructed on a fault line. He explained that over a fault line, the earth's magnetic field is very strong. And where the magnetic field is strong, spirits seemed to be more prevalent. He went on to explain that radon gas could be escaping from the ground and seeping through the floor boards. This radon gas could cause a reaction from the brain which would trigger such sightings.

The first thing a scientist always does is try to find a scientific explanation for the unexplainable. Heidi was born with a veil as was her maternal grandmother. What other explanations do we need? Some things just are.

20

THE STUDY CONTINUES

The following week, the Wyricks granted permission for Dr. Roll to continue his study of their daughter in hopes that he could help. They also gave permission for a national television show, acting on a tip from Dr. Roll, to air their story. The "haunted house" on Swint Loop began to draw public attention.

For the Wyricks this created a different kind of nightmare. An onslaught of national and international phone calls began, continuing day in and day out, week after week. Letters began pouring in from all over the world, each with a different agenda. Among them were curiosity-seekers; the grief stricken wanting to know if Heidi could contact their loved ones; others who claimed they could help. A daily entourage of vehicles began circling the block slowing or stopping briefly in front of their house.

Television and newspaper reporters clamored for exclusive rights to the story. Local television news ran the story on prime time and late night. Human interest ran high. More problems arose.

Entire churches turned out on the lawn, circling the house, candles lit, praying for the house, praying for the family. All walks of faith turned out for the purpose of exorcising evil spirits from the house. Outside prayers continued into the night. Inside the Wyricks felt comforted.

Dr. Roll's investigation continued. He'd validated the haunting in his own mind after Heidi had correctly identified pictures of the two men. But he wanted more evidence. He would be here tomorrow morning with some of his staff to further his study.

Heidi saw a car pull into the driveway and watched as Dr. Roll stepped out. There was a man and a woman with him whom she didn't recognize. She watched as Dr. Roll opened the trunk of the car and the other man lift out a huge box.

"Momma. We've got company."

It must be Dr. Roll, Lisa thought. *He said he'd be here at seven-thirty.* She glanced at her watch. He was right on time.

Lisa stepped out onto the front porch. "Good morning," she said.

"Yes, good morning." Dr. Roll smiled and introduced his staff. "I'd like you to meet Claire and Damon. They are students from the Department of Psychology and work with me part time. Both of them are very interested in this case."

Lisa smiled, reaching out to shake hands. They were both young, probably in their early twenties. Claire was beautiful. Her olive complexion and dark eyes complimented her dark brown hair. Damon, on the other hand, was blond, pencil thin and wore round glasses.

"It's really nice to meet ya'll," she smiled, pulling Heidi close. This is Heidi."

"Hello Heidi. I'm glad to finally meet you. I've heard a lot about you from Dr. Roll," Damon said.

"Me, too," the woman said, smiling warmly.

"Hello Heidi." Dr. Roll had already become very fond of her. "How are you today?" He ruffled her hair.

"Good."

"How's Wolf?"

"He's good, too."

"Outstanding."

Damon opened the box and handed Dr. Roll a round, clocklike gauge that resembled a compass. "This is a state-of-the-art electromagnetic field meter." He pointed to the needle on the gauge. "If there are areas where the normal magnetic field is high or disrupted, this needle will indicate it. What I'd like to do is place them in several locations around the house, leave them overnight and come back tomorrow to collect the data."

"How do these meters work?" Lisa asked.

"Well, according to the latest research, spirits are electromagnetic in origin. A presence will cause a disruption in the magnetic field, which is then recorded on the meter. It will record the time and strength of the disruption as well." Doctor Roll might as well have been talking gibberish.

Lisa spoke up, "I don't know what you just said but I hope it works."

Heidi and Lisa watched as they placed the equipment strategically throughout the house.

Two hours later, Dr. Roll was satisfied with the placement of five units in areas of the house where Heidi claimed to have had sightings.

Dr. Roll collected his data and machinery the next day. His face was flushed with excitement. The meters had spiked to some of the highest levels he'd ever seen, further authenticating what he already knew.

The investigation still wasn't over. Dr. Roll suggested that he bring in two well-known mediums, both from the Parapsychology Department at prestigious universities—one from Florida and the other from out West. He was very enthusiastic about this particular case and wanted to exhaust every avenue of research possible.

He arrived with the psychics two weeks later. His rules were very strict regarding the readings. The psychics could not discuss their own unique abilities with each other. They would have to work independently at the Wyrick home. They were not allowed to meet or even see the family until after the findings were concluded and well documented. Dr. Roll had elected to tell them nothing in advance and that's the way the psychics wanted it. That was the way they worked best.

Dr. Roll called that morning to let the Wyricks know he was on the way. He also requested that they leave the house until the investigation was over. He didn't want the psychics' opinions skewed in any way and if they met the family it might interfere with the readings.

Lisa, Andy and Heidi decided to stay next door at Joyce's. They watched from the bedroom window as Dr. Roll's car pulled in the driveway. Two women exited the car and immediately began to peruse the premises. One was tall and thin, her coal-black hair hung down her back, her bangs cut straight across. She was smoking a cigarette. She was weird looking even at a distance. The other female was short in stature and wore a long, ruffled skirt with bright colors of red, yellow and blue. She didn't turn around.

Dr. Roll and the shorter woman stepped inside while the tall, thin one walked around the side of the house toward the chimney. She turned abruptly toward Joyce's house gazing directly toward the window where they stood.

"Close the curtain!" Andy said. He was either skeptical or scared. He didn't want them in his house, but Lisa insisted.

"She's not looking at us." Lisa closed the curtains leaving just enough space for them to see out.

Heidi walked away from the window. Lisa was worried about her. She was only eight years old. She knew the psychics were coming. They'd discussed it at length before they agreed to give it a try.

"Lisa, look," Joyce said. Lisa pulled the curtain up and peeked out. The dark-haired woman was gesturing with her hands—red lips moving as though speaking to someone. Her tall, thin body seemed to stiffen, then go limp. Lisa felt the hair stand up on her arms. The woman lingered close to the chimney for a while then moved toward the back yard and eventually out of sight.

Inside the house, Dr. Roll followed the other psychic, jotting down notes quickly as she moved from room to room. She started down the hall toward the bedrooms and became terrified as a strong force physically knocked her backwards.

Stunned at what she felt, she shrieked, "I can't go in there!" Her eyes were closed, as if in a trance. She spoke slowly, her words deliberate.

"It's just too strong. It doesn't want me in there." She trembled. "The presence is evil, demonic." She cocked her head to one side as if to listen. "No, I won't." She began to back away, slowing at first, and then turned to run. She didn't stop until her feet hit hard soil.

Dr. Roll had seen many things, but this was a first. He'd worked with a lot of mediums but had never seen one run from the situation. He didn't ask questions. When you worked with a medium, you just stood by and listened. He'd learned that. When they were in their element, they were not to be disturbed.

The dark-haired woman entered the house. As soon as she stepped through the front door, Dr. Roll sensed her fear—just as he had with the first medium.

"There is a malignant influence in this house," she said. "It's cunning, and make no mistake about it, it can inflict physical harm. Be careful, be very careful."

Lisa and Joyce were riveted to the window staring out nervously. They both wished they could have heard what the psychics had to say first hand. However, it was a long while before Dr. Roll summoned the family, ready to reveal the findings.

The inexplicable facts were remarkable as both psychics had encountered some of the same entities. Both of them were unwilling or unable to enter the Wyrick's bedroom because negative vibes were so strong. They separately reported that something so evil resided in that room that they felt physically threatened.

Both women reported seeing several spirits, including a young girl, seven or eight years of age, outside the home. They agreed that normally ghosts haunted the inside of houses and buildings and that spirits roaming outside was very unusual in the world of psychic phenomena. The eeriest thing they reported was that the chimney was a doorway. The chimney where Heidi often played as a young child and the place she was so enthralled with the day they moved in, was now identified as the portal, a gateway where the spirits transcended to and from our world and theirs.

Now, armed with this information, what would they do with it? They couldn't stop it. The spirits that lurked here had been verified, but that's it, verified! Verification of what they'd already suspected was of no real value, unless, of course, they sold out and moved. But Lisa felt that this was not the answer. In her heart she knew that wherever they went, the spirits would follow.

The only hope was prayer. She believed that. Prayer was a part of her—a part of her family. Only the good Lord could change things. She'd talk with Andy and see if he'd agree to discuss this with their pastor. But even so, today was Monday, and Sunday seemed like an eternity away.

21
Bizarre Occurrences

In the pre-dawn hours Friday morning a soft knock at the front door caused Heidi to open her eyes. Still relaxed, she shut them again but continued to listen.

There it went again, louder this time.

She stumbled out of bed and into the living room where Andy and Lisa slept these days. Andy felt more comfortable there.

"Momma," Heidi shook Lisa. "Momma, wake up. Somebody's knocking on the front door."

"What?" Her voice was groggy."

"Momma, somebody's at the door. I've heard'em knock twice. Please get up and see who it is." Heidi's voice was pleadingly insistent.

"I didn't hear anything." Lisa sat up rubbing her eyes.

"Are you sure it was the front door?"

"Yeah, I'm sure."

Lisa squinted and looked at the bright red numbers on the clock. "Who in the world would be knocking on the door at three in the morning?" she asked."

"Andy, get up. Somebody's here." She shook him hard. "Get up."

"Ain't nobody out there." He rolled over.

"Heidi said she heard'em knock twice."

"Ya'll just hearin' things. Go back to sleep."

"Daddy, please just go look."

"Alright I'll look. But I'm tellin' you, ain't nobody out there." He got up, straightened his pajama bottoms and opened the front door.

"Who is it?" Heidi asked, hanging on to Andy's shirt tail.

"Nobody." He shut the door. "See, I told you. Now go back to bed. It's almost time for me to get up." Andy staggered back to the couch and was snoring within minutes.

"Heidi, you can sleep in here by us if you want to. I'll make you a pallet on the floor."

"Okay, but what about Jordan?" Heidi worried about Jordan constantly. She was eight years older and was always trying to *mother* her.

Lisa got up to check on her. She was sleeping peacefully. "She's okay. She's fast asleep."

Lisa sat on the recliner—she was wide awake now. She sat there until five o'clock before she got up to put on a pot of coffee for Andy. He always left the house by five-forty-five. After he left she showered and sat down at her dressing table, staring into the mirror at her swollen eyelids, thinking that no makeup in the world would conceal those dark circles.

She picked up the bottle of makeup and was unscrewing the cap when she heard Wolf growl. She sat motionless, listening. Then she heard it again. A peculiar feeling crept over her. Suddenly she got a whiff of stench so obnoxious she began to get nauseous. It smelled like a dead animal. She couldn't tell where it was coming from. She didn't have time to drag everything out of the closet this morning. She'd get Andy to check later.

She heard Wolf again. It sounded as if it was coming from under the house, directly under where she was sitting. *Okay*, she thought, *this is nerve racking*.

The barking became more frantic, and then she heard the voice of a woman trying to quiet the dog. "Come on boy, be quiet, shush … shhh." The voice was low, almost to the point of a loud whisper. Then the voice said, "Shhh boy, its okay."

The hair on her body bristled. *My Lord, why would anyone be under the house this time of morning? Its pitch dark out there,* she thought. She took a deep breath, picked up a flashlight from the chest of drawers and went outside.

The house was built on pier and beam so there was crawl space between the ground and floor. She started around to a small maintenance door on the side of the house, making several passes across the yard with the flashlight beam. She had to *make* herself open the door and shine the light under the house. She passed the light into every corner from top to bottom. There was absolutely nothing under there. She felt as though she was caught in a spider web and one day the carnivore would quit playing and come in for the kill.

Panic sent her running, stubbing her toe on a rock in the process. Hopping on one foot, she made it to the back door and inside the house. She slammed the door shut and locked it. She was scared; her heart racing. As she stood with her back against the door she was taken back to the time she'd heard the voices in her bedroom.

The day seemed to have no end. At 5:00 PM Lisa hit the time clock and headed for her car. It'd been hard to keep her mind on her work. She kept thinking of the voices she'd heard this morning. Her job had done little to assuage her thoughts. What was the meaning of it? Why was she being tortured? Was the knocking Heidi heard at three o'clock this morning related to this incident? Lord God, do help.

She'd stopped at the grocery store then picked up Jordan from daycare. There was never enough time in the day to do everything that needed doing. She didn't get anything done this morning after the ordeal with the barking dog, and she had a lot to do around the house.

Jordan fell asleep in her car seat and didn't wake up when Lisa got her out. After putting her to bed she changed into sweats and started cleaning. Right away she noticed the obnoxious smell from this morning was mysteriously gone. She thanked God for that. She dragged out the old Hoover and began vacuuming the hallway.

The air seemed cooler in Jordan's room. She stepped in and then out of the room a couple of times, comparing the temperature. It was definitely cooler. *Hmm, that's weird,* she thought. She picked up a pair of shoes and went to put them in closet. As she did an apparition appeared, moving from inside the closet toward the bed. Lisa was paralyzed. She couldn't turn her eyes away. She watched helplessly as the figure of a woman, hauntingly beautiful and at the same time repulsive, moved closer to Jordan's bed where it began to crystallize and dissipate right before her eyes. Then, like a vapor from a pot of steaming water, she was gone—gone as though she was never there.

Lisa was shaking. She grabbed her sleeping baby and ran outside. The hot Georgia sun couldn't even warm her. *I can't go on much longer*, Lisa thought for the hundredth time. It seemed as though Sunday would never come.

22

A Cry For Help

The Wyricks attended church on Sunday morning and hung around after the service hoping to speak privately with their pastor. Lisa had made arrangements with Ester to take the girls home with her. When the last of the congregation had left they nervously approached him.

"Brother Shep, I was wondering if we could talk to you for a few minutes." Lisa asked.

One eyebrow shot up as he answered. "Of course, that's what I'm here for." He had a huge smile that lit up his whole face. It had a way of putting people at ease.

They followed him to a small office at the back of the church. When they were seated he looked inquiringly at both of them.

"I don't know where to start," Lisa said, looking at Andy.

"It's always best to start at the beginning," Brother Shep said, leaning back in his chair. "Take your time."

When Andy didn't say anything, Lisa began. "Something evil is in our house, Brother Shep, so evil we have been physically threatened. We don't know what to do. We need help." Lisa seemed depleted of energy and her hands actually shook.

"What's happened?" he asked, his eyes narrowing.

Lisa and Andy briefly recounted some of the more horrific events that happened at their house, phenomena that threatened them and their children.

"From what you're telling me, it sounds as though your family is under demonic attack and I can assure you, that's a force to be reckoned with. You should have come to us sooner. You can't fight something like that alone. I'll talk with Brother Fred and let him know what's been happening. We'll get the elders of the church to fast and pray with us. When we feel ready, we'll come to your house."

Lisa and Andy nodded, a seed of hope planted. None of the church members knew about the hauntings, the evil attacks. The Wyricks felt uncomfortable talking about it to anyone outside the family, but now they were desperate.

§

"Thanks for comin'." Andy ushered the two preachers into the living room. It had been almost a week since the meeting with Brother Shep and both he and Lisa had been very anxious. They didn't know what to expect.

"Why don't ya'll tell us a little bit more about what's been happening to you?" the preacher said. "I'd like Brother Fred to hear it directly from the two of you."

"Andy and Lisa began to piece together a story that was astonishing; their emotional appeal for help heartbreaking."

Neither preacher was shocked. They'd heard of this kind of activity before. Brother Fred spoke up, "The Bible teaches us that these kinds of demons can only be dealt with by fasting and prayer. Only God can help in these kinds of situations." He paused. "You know," he looked at Lisa, then Andy, "God says where two or more are gathered in my name, I will be in the midst, so I'd like to start by praying for the family. Let's hold hands and agree in one accord." The preacher bowed his head and the others followed his cue.

"Lord, shadows in this house bring terror and unhappiness to this family. Dispel any evil, God, with your love, and shelter this family in the shadows you provide—in a place where they will be safe and free in Jesus' name. Amen."

They all stood up. "We'll bless the house now beginning in the hallway, if that's okay, and then proceed to each room," Brother Shep said, opening his Bible.

Lisa nodded her head and slipped her arm through Andy's. "That would be wonderful. Thank you."

She and Andy remained in the living room; their heads bowed as they listened to the prayers and anointing. She could hear the Preacher's voice, "Let all bitterness and wrath and anger and clamor, and evil be put away from this house. We ask that this house be cleansed through and through, in the name of the Father, the Son and of the Holy Ghost."

Both preachers walked through the entire house, stopping to pray over every room, then stepped outside and prayed there. They prayed over the front door, the back door and all the outside walls, placing their hands on all surfaces as they went, anointing them with oil. They prayed long and hard for God's protection, that whatever lurked in the shadows of this house would leave the Wyrick family alone.

"I believe the house is clean," Brother Shep said when they were done. "I don't feel the resistance I felt when I arrived."

"I feel the same," Brother Fred chimed in. "I have to tell you that when I walked into this house I had a bad feeling—a strong, negative feeling. But thank the Lord, I don't feel that now."

Brother Shep said, "We have to stand up to the wiles of the devil. He'll do all he can to pull God's children down." He glanced around the living area. "By the way, where in the world did you get this beautiful, old piano?" He ran his hands along the ivory keys. "I'd love to try it out before I leave, if you wouldn't mind."

"Of course I don't mind. I'd love for you to play." Lisa said. She'd heard him play many times in church and he played beautifully. "I bought it from a friend of my momma's when Heidi started piano lessons last year."

He sat down and began to play some old gospel hymns—the kind of hymns that soothe the body and soul. He finished with a chorus of "Amazing Grace."

"Thanks for everything," Andy said, as he shook hands with both men.

"Well, thank you for letting me *tickle the ivories*," he said. He was trying to lighten the air a bit. "Seriously, Andy, don't hesitate to call us anytime, day or night."

Andy stood in the doorway until the two men reached the car and drove off.

He saw Lisa had been crying. "It's gonna be alright, Lisa. I believe it's all over now."

"I hope your right."

They clung to each other tightly, thinking thoughts of the innocent—*It's over now; everything's going to be* alright. Only it wasn't.

23

THE MAN IN PLAID

Joyce heard the school bus making its way down Swint Loop past her house. She heard the familiar squealing brakes as it came to a halt to let Heidi off. Joyce and her future daughter-in-law, Caroline, were curled up on the couch catching up on news. Caroline had been away at college for the past four years and they had a lot to talk about.

Realizing it was getting late and Niki and Richard would be home soon, she got up to start dinner. Caroline got up to help. It seemed like the minute they stepped into the kitchen there was a noise so deafening they thought a bomb had gone off. The entire house shook, rattling dishes in the kitchen cabinet.

"What in the hell was that?" Caroline yelled.

"I don't know." Joyce ran toward the front door, Caroline tagging close behind. She snatched the front door open. The swing on the front porch swayed lazily in the breeze. A hummingbird flapped its tiny wings as it sucked nectar from the feeder hanging from the eve of the house. All was calm.

They could hear the bus slowing down to turn, gears grinding. Heidi was standing by the mailbox staring toward her aunt's house. Lisa was yelling something from the front porch. They both waved when they saw Joyce and Caroline.

"What was that loud noise, Lisa?" Joyce called out.

"What noise, I didn't hear anything." Lisa shrugged her shoulders.

How could she not have heard that, Joyce thought, *as loud as it was?* Fort Benning was the largest infantry base in the United States but it was thirty-five miles from the house. You could hear distant explosions when they were practicing but they'd never even felt a tremor this far out, much less had dishes in the cabinets rattle. Whatever it was sounded as if it was a direct hit to the front of her house, and oddly enough, she and Caroline were the only ones who heard it.

"I'll be down in a little while." They went back inside and closed the door. After careful inspection of the inside they found nothing awry except pictures hanging slightly out of kilter on the walls. They turned on the television but saw no reports of any explosions in the area.

That evening after dinner, the kids left and Joyce walked over to Lisa's house as she often did in the evenings.

"Aunt Joyce, a man was on your front porch today," Heidi told her.

"When was that?"

"When I got off the bus," she said, matter-of-factly.

"No one knocked on the door. Caroline was there all afternoon." Joyce said. She was confused.

"What did he look like?"

"He was wearing khaki-colored pants and a red plaid shirt. He stood there for a minute, and then walked right through the wall."

Calculating from the time she heard the bus brakes squeal until she and Caroline heard the loud explosion, it was safe to say the two events were connected. The entity moving through solid matter must have caused a sort of shock wave resulting in a noise akin to a sonic boom. That was the only conclusion she could come up with. One thing was for sure, there would be no sleeping in this house tonight. She was unnerved, deprived of courage. Tension had its talons in her neck like a vise grip and she'd be by herself tonight.

"Stay with us tonight," Lisa suggested.

"I think I'd rather take my chances at my own house, if you know what I mean."

Lisa chuckled, but she knew quite well what Joyce meant.

§

The house on the other side of Joyce's was empty. Nature had taken over. Weeds in the back yard were almost as high as the storage shed. It had apparently been empty for some time. Miss Wilma and her son Ernest lived in the house next to it. Joyce had been friendly with Miss Wilma since she moved into her house on Swint Loop. She looked in on her whenever she had a chance. Miss Wilma's husband had been dead for about ten years and Ernest was an incurable drunk, stumbling in and out of the house without consistency, sometimes sober, other times drunk as an old coot.

Today Miss Wilma answered the door in her house dress. Her solid white hair was cut short, tufted up in the back like a duck's tail, as though she spent most of her time leaning back in her recliner. She was so pleased to have a visitor it made Joyce feel guilty that she hadn't been to see the old woman in a while.

"Come on in." A grin spread across her face, causing wrinkles to deepen.

Joyce judged her to be around sixty-five years old. It was difficult to say. She followed her into the living room. Miss Wilma's crochet work was everywhere. Doilies adorned the arms of the chairs. An afghan was spread over the back of the flowered sofa. A delicately hand crocheted creation on the end table was starched and ironed—the inner row standing up around the base of the lamp. I guess all this needlework gives her something to do, Joyce thought.

Miss Wilma plopped down on one end of the couch. "Sit right here next to me," she patted the couch cushion.

Joyce sat down. "How have you been, Miss Wilma? I've been trying to get over here for a couple of weeks now, but one thing after another came up and this is the first chance I've had to stop by."

"I've been doing pretty good, all things considered," she smiled warmly. She picked up her project and began crocheting.

"How's Ernest?"

"Drunk as a skunk most of the time." Miss Wilma didn't look up. "But he's a good boy deep down and he *is* a bit of company now and then."

Lisa and Andy knew Ernest well. He'd hitch a ride to town with Andy sometimes. Other times he'd pay Andy to take him.

"Well, I guess no matter what he does, he's still your son," Joyce said. "Never give up on him."

"Yeah, there for a while I thought he was straightening up." The hooked needle moved fast as she interlocked and looped the thread.

"I told Ernest. I said, Son, your Daddy visited me the other day and he was wearing the same old clothes he always wore, that same old pair of khakis and that same old red plaid shirt." Her hands moved faster—interlock-loop—interlock-loop.

Joyce tried to act nonchalant as she asked, "When was that, Miss Wilma?"

"About three weeks ago I s'pect."

Joyce held her trembling hands tightly together in her lap. "That's odd about the clothes. You mean to tell me he wore the same thing every day?"

"Just about. When they'd get dirty he'd take them off long enough for me to wash'em and he'd put 'em right back on. He was sick, you know. He told me many times that plaid flannel shirt was the most comfortable garb he owned." She looked up, "That was about six months before he passed on. Dropped dead right where you're sitting." She laid the work in her lap, grabbed a tissue from the end table and dabbed her eyes.

It was all Joyce could do not to get up and run. "If you don't mind my asking, did he actually die in those clothes?"

"Same ones, yes ma'am. Died right there of a massive heart attack. I wanted to bury him in them but Ernest wouldn't let me. I still keep'em though, hanging right there in the closet. I guess when I'm dead, Ernest can do something with'em." She dabbed her eyes again. "I miss him. Yes ma'am, I sure do miss'im."

"You need anything, anything at all Miss Wilma, you just let me know." She stood up.

"I'm alright. I got Ernest. He's really not as bad as people think." She put her crochet work aside and stood up.

"I wish you could stay longer, but I understand if you have to go."

"I do have to run, but I'll come back first chance I get."

Joyce practically ran to her car. Sitting behind the steering wheel, she couldn't muster up the strength to turn the key. There was no getting around it. The description fit and so did the time frame. It was Miss Wilma's husband Heidi saw on her front porch. That was the man who walked right through her living room wall. She needed to talk to Lisa. *Dear Lord, help us all!*

24

SKEPTICS

Circumstances change sometimes without warning. Joyce was moving. Lisa was losing a lifeline and Heidi had grown into a young lady. Joyce and Greg Cathey's destiny was sealed the first time they met over a year ago, a predetermined course of events already set in motion. A mutual love, respect and devotion soon sent them to the church to be joined in marriage. Their new home was being built on the other side of the county. It was indeed a gray day for Lisa's entire family.

But the old cliché "when one door closes another always opens" proved correct when Andy's parents, Jack and Jane Wyrick, bought the house from Joyce—one parent a believer, the other a skeptic.

Jane cried for Heidi every night but Jack closed his eyes to the fact that his granddaughter had a sixth sense. "Yeah, yeah, yeah," Jack would say if she mentioned her ghostly encounters, and he'd laugh. Heidi was hurt that Granddaddy didn't believe her. He didn't realize how sad it made her feel. She knew her granddaddy loved her, but also knew that a lot of people were afraid of the spirit world. She believed he was one of them. But, you have to be careful what you laugh at—laughter can easily turn into crying.

Jack stood near the fireplace at his son's house holding Jordan on one hip and talking with Heidi about her upcoming piano recital. She had been taking lessons for a year and was doing well. She had a natural talent.

"Granddaddy, I've been working real hard on a piece I'll be playing at the recital. Wanna hear it?"

Before Jack could say a word Heidi began screaming, "Let go of me! Stop it! Let go of my hair!"

Jack looked up astonished as he witnessed a phenomenon so terrifying that it would be stamped in his memory forever. Heidi's ponytail was being pulled, straight out, by unseen hands, her head jerked back. The roots of her hair were pulled taut. And there was nothing Jack could do. He couldn't move. He felt a scream in the pit of his belly that couldn't be released. *My Lord, this is what the kids had been talking about!*

Again, Heidi shouted, "Stop pulling my hair!"

The paralysis lifted. Jack shouted for Lisa and Jane but by the time they got to the living room, the hair pulling had stopped and Heidi was crying.

"I saw Heidi's head being pulled backwards. Something practically lifted her off the floor by her ponytail and there was nothing I could do." Jack's eyes were brimming with tears. "It's too horrible to talk about," His head was bent, his fingers raking through salt-and-pepper hair.

"I hate this house," Heidi wailed through her tears. "I hate it, I hate it!" She ran to her room, fell across her bed, and sobbed into her pillow. Why did this happen to her, why?

Jack came into her room and sat down on the edge of her bed. "Oh granddaddy, I wish I could just move away. I'm so tired of all this. I want so badly to be like everyone else."

Jack rubbed her head. "I'm so sorry, Heidi. I'm so sorry." He was sorry for many things … that this kind of torment was heaped on a young girl, not to mention her Momma and Daddy. And he was sorry he'd had to see for himself before he could believe and support them when they most needed it. What he hated most was that he'd laughed. He hadn't believed a word of it until this moment. And now he knew it was true.

"I hate the fact that I see things—unexplained things. I'm tired of the other kids laughing and making fun of me." Heidi sobbed. "I pray every day that God will just take it away."

Heidi sat up and wiped tears from her face. She saw Lisa standing in the doorway. She was crying, too. "It's alright, Momma. I'm fine now." Heidi was old enough, mature enough, to know that her *gift* not only affected her, but her whole family. She walked over and put her arms around her mother.

"Granddaddy, can we go to your house for a while?"

Before he could answer they were distracted by a loud thumping noise coming from the hallway.

"What's that noise?"

"I don't know," Jack said. "Sounds like it's coming from the bathroom."

Crying on the other side of the door brought Jack running. "It's Jane," he said.

Lisa grabbed the door knob and it turned easily in her hand. "What's wrong with this door? It's not locked," she said. "Jane, pull on the door." Her mother-in-law was not well. It wouldn't do to leave her in there for very long.

Jane pulled and Jack pushed. The door didn't budge.

"Get me out of here!" A breathless sob followed. Jane was claustrophobic. The walls were closing in on her and she felt a panic attack coming on. She was beginning to hyperventilate.

"Jane, back away from the door. I'm gonna bust it in!" Jack had seen his wife have panic attacks and couldn't bear to see her suffer.

"Hurry!" Jane yelled, as she moved quickly toward the opposite wall. Just as Jack got ready to kick the door in, it began slowly opening on its own. Everybody looked on in disbelief.

What in the world was going on? Lisa thought. *Something's showing me it's got control.* It was as if the incident was a power-play, that maybe something beyond her understanding was showing its authority. She could feel cold air from the bathroom start at her feet and continue up her legs.

Jane came out crying. "It was like someone or something strong was holding the door. I've never been so scared. My nerves are shot to pieces. I'm going on home and lay down."

Heidi stayed that night with her grandparents. She stayed for herself and her Nanny Jane. And sometimes she just felt safer at Nanny Jane's than she did in her own home. Tonight she needed to feel safe.

25

UNKNOWN TONGUES

The blackest hours are right before dawn, midnight of the soul. The hours between one and four are the lowest point for the human body, when it is least able to fight off crisis, when it's as close to death as it'll get without actually dying. It stands to reason that spirits would more commonly wander the premises during these hours or that a demonic attack would come when you are mentally and physically at your lowest. That's what happened to Lisa.

Lisa had just gotten in bed. She'd been studying her Sunday school lesson. Andy and the girls had been asleep for some time and it was extremely quiet. As she began to relax she heard a harsh, throaty sound coming from somewhere in the bedroom. Goose pimples covered her body as the sounds became louder and she could make out two distinctive voices. Low, guttural voices began speaking in a language she didn't recognize, back and forth across the bed. She felt helpless and horror stricken. She felt as though they were discussing *her*, that a diabolical scheme was being plotted against her life. She was totally paralyzed. Andy was sound asleep right beside her and she couldn't move her arm to shake him awake.

The God-awful gibberish continued. It was more terrifying than her worst nightmare, yet she was awake. She opened her mouth to scream but no sound came forth. In her mind she beseeched the entity to be gone in the name of Jesus.

The infernal voices began to resonate, bouncing off the walls. She began to plead the blood of Jesus over and over in her mind. As the paralysis lifted, she reached out and grabbed her Bible from the bedside table. It was her anchor in the time of storm. Some pages were loose, others worn thin with use. She opened it and laid it across her chest.

The Bible clearly states that demons are at work in the spiritual realm and that we, as Christians, are very much involved in a battle against the ruler of darkness—the destroyer of men's souls.

She began to pray quietly at first, but the voices seemed to be mimicking her, gradually increasing in force and volume. She began to pray out loud, "Yea, though I walk through the valley of the shadow of death, I will fear no evil: for thou art with me ..."

She heard snickering. It was bone chilling.

She prayed louder and louder and as she did, a feeling of strength and determination began to flow through her veins—a surge of courage like never before coursed through her. She knew it was from God. She began to rebuke the demons, "Leave this house right now in the name of Jesus Christ!" Her voice became more demanding, "I bind you Satan from my house and my family, in the name of Jesus Christ. Get out!" She was no longer crying.

It sounded like thunder rattling the very window panes, like the storm of the century, as they left.

Then there was silence and peace descended upon her. The relentless enemy of mankind had invaded her house, had emotionally assaulted her and with the Lord's help she had won. She didn't realize she was weeping until she tasted the clear salty liquid on her lips.

"Thank you, Lord," she whispered, then switched on the bedside lamp and began reading her Bible.

Beside her, Andy still slept soundly. She didn't wake him. What was the use, now? They'd already gone.

She didn't know if she'd ever sleep again. She had been that scared. She'd arm herself with a Bible in every room. She'd be read up and prayed up, because she felt the great deceiver had been there that night and would certainly be back. He didn't go after those who were already his victims. His greatest pleasure was defeating all that was Holy. Joyce always told her, *if you don't meet the devil on your walk with the Lord, you're going the same way he is.* Oh yes, he'd be back.

26

Sister Lovie

Heidi was sixteen years old now and in no way had her special abilities diminished. However, she *was* learning to cope. The Wyricks were a Christian household and turned more and more toward their faith for solace, comfort and emotional support; in turn, the church welcomed them into its fellowship. They began attending three times a week—twice on Sunday and Wednesday night prayer meeting. Although they read the Bible daily, preaching and singing inspired them and uplifted their spirits.

But for Heidi there was another main attraction. His name was Aaron. She was usually reserved, almost timid, especially around the opposite sex. But there was something about Aaron—maybe it was his magnetic charm that made her feel special. They usually sat on opposite sides of church with their families, but she'd catch his eye occasionally and she knew the attraction was reciprocated. She felt almost giddy. Aaron was a tall, handsome young man with dark hair and blue eyes.

As it turned out Aaron was as bashful as Heidi, so for a long time their relationship was limited to glances and subtle smiles at church. Heidi's Aunt Ester noticed and decided to give the relationship a push by boldly inviting Aaron to go with them to an outside play near Atlanta. It was the beginning of a serious relationship.

The church was packed this morning; there was standing room only at the back of the small sanctuary. Sister Lovie LaRoche beamed as the preacher asked her to come forward and sing a 'special.' Lovie was a mulatto, born in New Orleans around 1931, her skin the color of creamy coffee. She rose from the pew moving toward the front of the church, her teal-colored hat sitting at a cocky angle on a crown of braided hair. Salt and pepper fuzz framed her face like fox fur. She was not a member of the church on Ferrell's Creek Road, but when she attended she was expected to sing, and sing she could. The rhythm of Negro heritage pulsated through her body as she made a joyful noise unto her Creator.

The pianist began banging out notes trying to find the right key as Lovie hummed. She was in her element. Microphone in hand, already swaying, she began:

> *Sis ... tah, oh sis ... tah*
> *De massa's got a plan fo' you*
> *Oh, yes he does*
> *De massa's got his eyes on you.*

Her head rolled back and her eyes were shut. She had a pained expression on her face, her thick lips spread wide, pressed against white teeth. Her song continued:

> *The massah—he done give you de pow ... ah*
> *Of healin' in yo hands*
> *Yes he placed the pow ... ah in you*
> *'Cause my massa's got a plan*
> *Oh, yes he does*
> *My massa's sho nuff got a plan.*

Thin legs spread out; knobby knees bobbing up and down; foot tapping; body moving in time with the music. She was worshiping her Maker as prophetic song bubbled up like a natural spring.

> *Sis ... tah, my sis ... tah*
> *De massa's got a job for you*
> *Oh, yes he does*
> *De massa's got his eyes on you.*

Church members were up now, marching up and down the aisles, tambourines shaking out metallic music, pelting out God's glory. An old-fashioned camp meeting jubilee was in session.

> *The massah he done give you discernment*
> *He give you pow ... ah ova devils in hell*
> *Pow ... ah to make sinners whole is in you*
> *Heah me now—you got a job to do*
> *Yeah girl, the massa's got his eyes on you.*

Everybody that wasn't marching stood up, clapping to the music. You could feel the Holy Ghost on the prowl. Lovie's body bounced to the music, left arm out straight, palm up, right index finger sweeping across the audience, stopping at Heidi.

> *Sis ... tah—heah me now*
> *My, my, my massa's got work for you.*
> *Heah me now*
> *De's a whole lot of work to do*

Heidi felt faint. The room tilted as Lovie's finger seemed to grow and come straight out through the audience and tap her on the chest above her heart. The music dimmed in her mind as though it was coming from far away. Across the aisle Heidi could see Pawpaw watching her. He'd known from the beginning that Heidi was special, and Memaw and Pawpaw were certainly special to her.

She could see Nanny Jane two rows up, clapping her hands in time with the music. Her Nanny had been sick and Heidi had been praying for her for days. She'd been very worried. Jane not only had Lupus, but a host of other health problems as well. Heidi's eyes squinted as she stared at Jane. Suddenly it was as if no one else was in the room and there was an extraordinary, unearthly light surrounding her. As she concentrated on the light it appeared to be gold prisms joined together falling like rain, enveloping Jane. It was phenomenal, truly awesome.

When the service was over, Heidi approached the pastor and told him about the curious celestial lights. Brother Shep explained about mercy rain; a miracle of biblical proportions because not many people, and only one that he knew of, had ever witnessed it. Mercy rain enveloped a person being healed, the rain being God's mercy toward them.

Heidi felt blessed; her heart warmed. She felt that God have given her the ability to lay hands on the sick and pray for them through Jesus Christ. Lovie had prophesied that over her. She was sure now that she was put on this earth to accomplish things beyond her understanding and no cord around her neck while still in the womb could have been victorious because God knew her then and he knew her now. He protected her then and he protected her now.

Heidi would be allowed to see mercy rain again and again, and her heart would rejoice.

27

Overnight Guests

Tugging at the back of Lisa's mind was the fact that the Catholic church still performed exorcism rituals. Several times over the years she'd toyed with the idea of talking to a priest although she was not of the Catholic faith. They were running out of options to deal with this thing. Several times she'd picked up the phone, only to lay it back in its cradle. Her family was exhausted. They went to bed dog-tired almost every night.

A few days ago a life-long family friend showed up at their house. Faith had compelled her to come and pray for the family, the house, and the situation. That evening when she was walking toward her car, she tripped over something, although she saw nothing was in her path. When she got into her car and started backing out of the drive she heard a distinct voice say, "You'll pay for this." In the following months, inexplicable things began happening to her—unnatural things that could in no way be accounted for. Lisa understood that they were dealing with a diabolical force—a force befitting hell. She decided to try and make the call again. Just as she reached for the phone it rang, causing her to jump.

It was Adam, Lisa's nephew. He, his wife Jennifer and their eighteen-month-old son Caleb was coming to spend the night. They were leaving to go home to Texas the next morning and wanted to spend some time with Lisa and Andy before they left.

Overnight company was indeed rare at the Wyrick's. It seemed like a blessing for people to actually spend the night. She decided to put them in Heidi's room since she was staying the night with Montein.

Lisa and Andy were planning on taking their company out for dinner until they heard the weather forecast. Storms were brewing to the west and they could get some rough weather by this evening. When Adam and Jennifer arrived they decided just to order pizza and stay home.

Dinner over, they sat on the front porch talking and watching storm clouds roll in. They could see jagged flashes of lightning in the distance and could hear an occasional rumble of thunder.

Jordan was inside playing with Caleb and had him laughing hysterically over her silly antics.

"We'll have to get inside in a few minutes," Andy said as the wind snatched the lid off the garbage can and carried it across the front yard.

"Come on, Jennifer, let's go on inside. It's getting too windy out here." Lisa got up and opened the screen door. "Anybody want something to drink?"

"I'll take some tea if there's any left," Adam said as he got up and followed them inside.

"Yeah, there's plenty left. I've got Coke, too, if you'd rather have it."

"Tea's fine," he said

"Man, that wind is really pickin' up," Andy said, as he shut the door and locked the door. "Lisa, pour me a glass of tea, too."

Adam started toward the bedroom to put on his sweatshirt. He felt chilled. When he got to the hallway, he noticed a long plume of what appeared to be a black, smoky substance being pulled into the air-conditioning vent. He looked at it perplexed, dismissing it after it vanished.

It was eleven-thirty by the time they settled down and got to sleep. Sometime after midnight Adam and Jennifer were both awakened by a noise. The sound was something between a groan and a sob and seemed to be coming from the far corner of the room. Neither one spoke. They heard it again. The third time they heard it, it sounded as though it was coming from the foot of the bed.

"Did you hear that, Adam?" Jennifer whispered.

"Yeah," he whispered back.

"What is it?"

"I don't know."

Jennifer reached out and turned on the lamp on the bedside table. They didn't see anything. Nothing seemed to be out of order.

Adam got up cautiously, moving around the room. He thought maybe the dog had somehow gotten in.

"That's weird," he said. "There's nothing in here."

Just as he sat down on the bed, he was attacked by a force he couldn't see. It grabbed his leg, flipping his whole body around before knocking him backwards onto the mattress, pinning him down.

He started punching and kicking in an attempt to free himself but he couldn't. He began screaming, "Get it off. Get it off."

Jennifer was so frightened she began screaming. It scared the baby and he began crying hysterically.

Andy came running. He halted at the doorway, too scared to enter the room. He could see that Adam was physically being held down, but he couldn't see his adversary. It was the most terrifying thing he'd ever witnessed. An all-out fight was in progress—one person visible; the other invisible.

Andy was frozen. His legs wouldn't move. "Li-sah-ah-ah," he shrieked.

She jumped from the bed and came running. A swift glance in the bedroom and she began praying as loud as she could, commanding whatever it was to leave.

Time seemed to stand still. Finally it was gone.

"Whatever it was felt damp and heavy—I couldn't breathe. For a minute, I thought I was going to die. I've never had anything like that happen to me before," Adam said, his lip still quivering.

Jennifer was still crying.

Lisa tried to calm both of them down but it was a nearly daylight before they all settled down again.

"I guarantee you one thing," Andy said. "Somethin' gits on me like that, I'm gone and I won't never come back. Man!" he shook his head.

No one would shut their eyes again this night. It was worse than horrible to see someone fight for his life with an unseen opponent—especially one so powerful. Adam was strong, but not strong enough to prevent being restrained by this dominating force—a force that had held him down without difficulty.

When morning came, Adam packed up his family and headed for home, never looking back.

§

The whole family laughed at Andy's re-enactment of Adam karate-kicking and punching the unseen entity with a fear-induced strength you rarely see. Especially Phillip, Lisa's youngest brother. But Lisa remembered not long ago when Phillip spent the night at their house, a terrible thing happened to him, too, something he wouldn't soon forget.

He and Andy planned on going hunting before daylight so they'd all gone to bed early. He woke up during the night feeling uncomfortably hot and got out of bed to adjust the thermostat. Lisa and Andy's bedroom was at the end of the hallway and they'd left the door open. He didn't want to wake them so he didn't turn on the light. It was pitch dark as he slid his hand along the wall feeling for the thermostat box. Out of the darkness, without warning, a voice spoke. It was a low moaning intonation in a tongue he'd never heard—nor ever wished to hear again. It was as if the voice spoke just behind his left ear. The hair on his neck and scalp prickled. He recoiled in horror. He had no earthly idea how long he stood there in that dark hallway, too terrified to move. He felt as though any minute he would hear a snicker.

The house became unnaturally quiet, but something was in there, in the shadows, watching. He could sense it, feel it. Eventually he was able to move toward the bedroom, then reaching out, he turned on the lights. Even then, he couldn't shake the eerie feeling. He lay back down on the bed and turned the radio on. He could hear his own heart pounding in his ears. He was hoping the music would block out any further sounds. Seconds later, the radio turned itself off! Two voices began to speak gibberish back and forth across his bed. The language, just as he'd heard in the hallway, was incomprehensible. Several minutes passed as the voices continued. But then it stopped.

If it wasn't in the middle of the night, he thought, *I'd get in my truck and leave.* He could go to his parents, but he'd hate to wake them. He lay there, covered up to his ears with a blanket—lights blaring in his eyes. Lisa needed to get out of this house. If it was him, he'd leave everything he owned and jump in his car and drive—drive as far away from this hell-hole as he could get. He'd tell her that in the morning. He calmed down a little, then reached over and turned the radio back on—seconds later, it turned itself off again.

He couldn't take it anymore. He got out of bed and woke Lisa. He needed to hear a human voice. It was almost time for Andy to get up, anyway.

"Lisa, wake up." She mumbled something. "I just wanted to tell you I turned the thermostat down." He knew she didn't care, but he wanted someone else awake in the house. It made him less nervous. He went back to bed but didn't close his eyes.

Lisa tried to go back to sleep but it was useless. *What was all that about?* she thought. *I wonder why he woke me up to tell me that?* She decided to get up and start the coffee. When she passed the room where Phillip was, she saw he was still awake.

"It's a good thing you got up," he said, clearly upset.

"Why?"

"Oh, nothing." He paused. "Has that radio got a timer on it that cuts it off?"

"No. It's just an AM/FM radio. Why?"

Over coffee, he told Lisa what had happened. It had literally scared the daylights out of him. The way he figured it, this house didn't want anybody else here; and one thing for sure, he'd never stay another night under this roof. This was the most harrowing experience of his life and not one that he'd forget—not as long as he lived.

28

SEARCH AND DESTROY

Lisa started planning a Forth-of-July party as soon as she found out her sister from Texas was coming. The family tried to get together as much as possible when she was here, and there would be plenty of food and drinks. Lisa loved having the family over but all of them were fearful of staying the night, especially after what happened with Adam and Phillip. It wasn't that something supernatural *might* happen—it was almost a sure thing that it *would*. So getting Becky to spend the night was totally out of the question.

Today they were just going to concentrate on being together and having fun. The atmosphere was alive with chatter, children laughing and running through the house. An enormous array of food sat on the dining room table. Heidi had even made a red, white and blue Jell-O cake decorated to look like a flag.

While the women stood in the house gossiping, the men were grouped out on the lawn in animated conversation. The dilemma was whether to pile up in cars and go to the fireworks display at Callaway Gardens or cross the Chattahoochee River into Alabama and buy fireworks. It was illegal to have fireworks in the state of Georgia, but local lawmen usually turned a deaf ear to a few firecrackers, especially outside the city limits. The trip to Alabama won out and Richard, Joyce's son, volunteered to drive. Within minutes they were in his Toyota headed for the state line—Andy in the front seat with him, Marcus and Phillip in the back.

Kids ran in and out of the house laughing and screaming, chasing each other around and around the house. They were having a ball. At dusk Lisa brought out the official lightning bug palace: a clean pickle jar with nail holes in the lids that would allow the bugs to breath. Now they were on a quest to catch enough lightning bugs to make a lantern.

Before long the men returned, unloading several bags of fireworks onto the front porch. It sure wasn't limited to firecrackers and sparklers. They must have bought one of every kind they had for sale, including bottle rockets. Bottle rockets make a loud whistle before they launch, making a loud explosive sound at about seventy five feet, sending multi-colored sparks on decent in an umbrella fashion. The display was beautiful in the dark, night sky. Something in the genes makes explosives very appealing to the male gender. They were more excited than the kids.

The kicker was the explosive Phillip had gotten from one of his Army buddies. It was a great deal larger than the ones they'd purchased and they had no idea what it would do. So Phillip told everyone to get out of the way. He lit the fuse and ran.

Nobody knows exactly what happened next. The bottle tipped over and started spinning, just like a gun on top an army tank. It began a slow swivel as if on a search-and-destroy mission, looking for a particular target. It locked in on Andy. The rocket exploded from the bottle with unbelievable force, hitting him slightly above the genital area, literally picking him up off his feet and throwing him backwards into the shrubbery.

Everybody was running toward Andy. Lisa was screaming his name. Richard pulled him from the shrubs. Andy's eyes were shut as though he was unconscious.

"Andy, Andy. Are you okay?" Lisa was rubbing his face.

His eyelids fluttered but he didn't speak.

"Ya'll help me get him inside." Richard, Marcus and Phillip picked him up and took him inside and laid him on the sofa; Lisa right behind them already checking for wounds. But other than being shook up and extremely red in his privates, he appeared to be alright. It was a miracle. That sort of an explosive could've killed him.

On reflection, no one that witnessed the bizarre incident that night could write it off as a mere coincidence. Knowing the history of the house, could it have been the destructive behavior of a malevolent spirit, the dark figure Heidi had seen? The launching area for the rockets was right next to the chimney where more than one psychic proclaimed it as a portal—an entry way from the spiritual world into the world of the living. It was a question that would always haunt every witness.

29
MANIFESTATIONS

Lisa, Andy and Jordan drove to town for dinner but Heidi had already made plans. She and Montein were meeting Aaron in town and he was bringing a friend to meet Montein. It was a double date and they were both looking forward to it.

Heidi had just stepped out of the bathroom and headed for the laundry room to retrieve a black GAP tee shirt from the dryer. She'd tossed it in earlier with a damp cloth to get the wrinkles out—a time-saving trick she'd learned from her mother. Just then the phone rang.

"Heidi, you ready?" It was Montein. "We're supposed to meet the guys in thirty minutes."

"Almost. I just need to get my shirt out of the dryer," Heidi said. "Honk the horn for me when you pull up and I'll meet you out front."

Heidi started down the hallway toward the laundry room but was startled by a little girl standing in front of the hearth. She appeared to be about seven years old. She stood spellbound, her heart in her throat, eyes drawn to the girl's face. Her unnaturally pale skin appeared powdered with hollowed dark eyes like liquid pools of black coffee. She looked at Heidi beseechingly, holding out one small hand. A halo of gold curls encased the small head, almost touching her waist. She had on a gingham dress with a sheer overlay that reached the top of her brown boots. Heidi's blood ran cold as an unwanted thought reared its ugly head, *dressed for eternity.* The little girl turned her eyes from Heidi and moved slowly toward the brick hearth—then, like a vapor, she vanished.

It was difficult for Heidi to keep her mind on the movie. She was obsessed by thoughts of the little girl. She had felt a strange connection with her somehow, something she couldn't explain.

That night after Heidi climbed into bed and pulled the sheets up around her, she lay awake for hours wondering about her visitor. *Was this girl the same one the psychics reported seeing outside?* Heidi wondered. *If so, what was it she was after?* Heidi tossed and turned. It bothered her because the spirit was a child. She hadn't even tried to communicate with her and she felt bad. Maybe she could've helped her.

She decided she wouldn't mention her to anyone. She had started keeping a lot of things to herself. There had been too much suffering and misery connected with her gift or curse, depending on how you looked at it.

Two weeks had passed since the incident with the girl, and although Heidi certainly hadn't forgotten it, she'd tried desperately not to let it dominate her thoughts. In fact, whenever it entered her mind she quickly starting singing out loud. If you were singing, you weren't thinking. Singing became one route of escape from her memories. She'd learned to cope by distracting herself.

Tonight was Wednesday night prayer meeting and Heidi was supposed to start dinner. She changed into her sweats and headed for the kitchen. As she rounded the corner, Heidi saw the little girl again. She was sitting on the ottoman in the den, dressed in the same clothes as before, hair hanging in curls to her waist. She didn't turn to look at Heidi this time. She just sat perfectly still, staring toward the window in the den. Heidi sensed a strong aura of hopelessness around her and it saddened her. She opened her mouth to speak but words wouldn't come. Moments later, the girl vanished, exactly as she had before.

Maybe I could help her if she'd talk to me, Heidi thought. *Maybe next time she will.*

Tomorrow she was going shopping with her Momma, Jordan and Montein. That thought cheered her up some. She walked over to her closet to figure out what she'd wear.

§

Heidi gazed up at the sky. Cumulus clouds looked like big balls of cotton drifting in the wind. It was amazing how fair weather clouds could quickly turn into heavy, ominous storm clouds. The same could be said of people. The majority stood by you only during the good times—they were "fair weather friends" who disappeared when life's storms moved in. She'd read somewhere, "*if you gain one true friend during a lifetime, consider yourself lucky.*" Montein was that friend.

Lisa eased the car onto the Manchester Expressway, accelerating to pass a Trinity Care handicap bus. Heidi sat in front with her mother; Montein and Jordan in back. Conversation and laughter flowed easily. Shopping and lunch were on the agenda for the day.

"Jordan wants Mexican. Is that okay with you, Montein?" Lisa asked.

"Yes Ma'am."

Heidi leaned back as Lisa moved into the right lane to exit.

Suddenly, a sound erupted from nowhere. It was unlike anything Heidi had ever heard. She jumped to the edge of the seat and looked around. It became louder. It sounded like a hundred flags flapping in hurricane-type winds. Her mother appeared to be talking to Jordan, but she couldn't hear them above the roar. She was badly frightened.

She jerked her head to the right as an enormous bird-like creature swooped down on the car, scraping its wing on the passenger window. It soared effortlessly alongside the car, as if it *wanted* to make sure she saw it. Sticks, insects and lint were caught in its feathers. It was filthy and repulsive—its wings a brownish-gray color like putrid, stagnant water. An overwhelming sense of evil oozed from its pores, poured from its empty eye sockets, smelling of death, hell and the grave. If not paralyzed she might have jumped from the moving vehicle to get away. As if in quicksand, all she could do was stare.

She couldn't speak. She could move her eyes, but she couldn't speak. Her fingers dug into the edge of the seat hard enough to leave permanent indentions. The other passengers were acting normal, as though they hadn't heard or seen anything. Heidi could see their mouths move, talking and laughing.

As the car began braking for a traffic light, the beast-like creature soared up to the top of a large office building poising itself with one wing across its face. The outline of the body seemed human—the wings a ten to fifteen foot span. What in the world was it, a bearer of bad news, an omen of some kind? Discernment of the spirit told her it was Lucifer himself—Heaven's adversary—showing his power, amusing himself with one of God's children as he had done since the beginning of time.

She closed her eyes and began to pray—"*Our Father who art in Heaven ...*" And as she inwardly recited the Lord's Prayer, she became stronger. When she looked up the demon was gone. But that wasn't the last time she'd see it.

30

An Unexpected Find

The day came when they packed up and left the house on Swint Loop. None of them wanted to look back. They were afraid of what they might see.

Over the course of years in that house they were plagued with illness—life-threatening illnesses. Jordan had been hospitalized ten times with severe bouts of asthma; three of those times were spent in the critical care unit. Heidi had gone through three surgeries, one of them being due to a ruptured appendix, and she almost died. Andy had three major surgeries and Lisa had two miscarriages. This didn't count all the times they'd had influenzas and other communicable diseases.

Family and friends encouraged them to move; all saying the same thing; "Get out of that house before it kills you." But they weren't financially able to move. Doctor and hospital bills ate up every penny they made and then some. They could barely make ends meet, much less come up with the money it would cost to move. It had taken fifteen years of saving pennies and a large income tax return to enable them to get out.

They escaped without incident—escaped the torment of apparitions, haunting and pure evil they'd experienced in that house over the past fourteen years. They felt free, as though they'd just been released from a prison cell.

The new house was just that, new. It had been completed only a month before they'd rented it. You could still smell fresh paint and new carpet. It would give them a new lease on life. Lisa set about using all her decorating skills to making it a home. With the few dollars they had left from the income tax check, Lisa decided to look for a new bed for Jordan, a full-size one in lieu of the twin bed she'd always used. She asked around but no one she knew had one for sale and she definitely couldn't afford a new one. She'd just have to share a room with Heidi until they run across one.

A week later a bed pretty much *found them*! On Sunday afternoon while driving home from church, Lisa spotted a garage sale sign by the road in front of an old Victorian home on Highway 85. She knew that house.

"Stop Andy," she yelled suddenly.

"No, I ain't stoppin'. You know that's the old Gordy House." The Gordy name held too many memories. The farther away from Ellerslie he could get, the better he liked it. At least now he could get a good night's sleep.

"Andy, please pull in there—please. You won't have to get out." Lisa insisted, so Andy reluctantly pulled the car off the road and onto the dirt drive. Lisa got out. She had to walk through a narrow opening in the hog-wire fence to get to the backyard where the sale was being held.

Two women sat under an old oak tree behind the screened-in back porch. Several tables held old lamps, dishes worn thin with use, an old photo album—nothing Lisa could use. A number ten washtub full of variegated ivy had taken over most of the yard, its roots like tiny fingers digging in and clinging to tree trunks, fences and plain hard dirt.

The younger of the two women got up, nodded briefly at Lisa, then went inside the old house. This place felt eerie.

She picked up a dish and started to ask the price but the old woman seemed unapproachable. She looked as ancient as the house. Her hair was tightly permed, her eyes as cold as steel. She caught Lisa looking at her.

"What is it you're looking for, Dearie?" as if she already knew.

Lisa wanted to politely escape, so she said the first thing that came to mind, "I've been looking for a bed for my daughter." She pointed to Jordan. "But I see you don't have one."

The way the old woman looked at her gave Lisa the creeps.

"Well now, you're quite the lucky one today." Her smile didn't reach her eyes. I've got a bedroom suite upstairs that I'd like to get rid of. Didn't feel like hauling it down the stairs by myself so I left it up there." Her voice creaked. "I guess it's just been sitting there waiting for you." She smiled again, making Lisa uncomfortable. "Come on in. I'll show you."

Lisa turned and motioned for Andy, but he shook his head. He wouldn't budge out of the truck. She reluctantly turned and followed the old woman into the house and up narrow stairs to the second floor; Jordan hanging on tight to Lisa's hand. Dim light peered through a stained glass window on the landing, but it was still dark enough to need a flashlight.

When the old woman turned the antique glass knob on the bedroom door and pushed it open, Lisa was astounded. She hadn't expected to see furniture of this caliber. It was gorgeous. Under the window was the most beautiful bed she'd ever laid her eyes on. There was a matching dresser and chest equally as beautiful. Upon quick examination, Lisa didn't find a marred spot on it. It appeared to be solid oak.

"If I can come up with the money, I'd really like to buy it."

She held her breath. She knew it was out of her league. But the old woman named a figure that was so mediocre that Lisa would have paid three times as much. She whipped out the cash and paid before the old woman had a chance to change her mind, then sent Jordan out to the car to fetch her daddy. She could hear Jordan's little footsteps as she ran hurriedly down the rickety staircase.

Andy and Lisa began to dismantle the bed—Andy grumbling the whole time that he was in a hurry to get to the woods.

The bed had been there so long the carved legs were stuck fast to the floor. Nobody had slept in it for a long time either, because the bedspread crunched as she pulled it loose from the old mattress. No telling how long it had stood in this room. After an hour, they'd finally hauled all the pieces down the staircase and onto the back of Andy's truck. Andy was tying it down with a rope the old lady had given him.

Lisa walked toward the woman, "Thank you so much, Ma'am." Lisa's heart was beating hard with excitement.

The woman divulged little personal information but did say that she'd purchased the house thirty years prior. Her husband passed away leaving her sole caretaker, and now she was putting in on the market.

"I'm glad you got the bed, child." She spoke in a low voice. "I wouldn't want just anyone to have it. It belonged to a man named Mr. Gordy." She bent her head slightly. Her gray eyes looking up at Lisa made the woman look wicked. Then she smiled.

Lisa's heart dropped. It was if the woman knew there was a connection. But Lisa would never have dreamed the furniture had actually belonged to him. She was speechless as she got into the truck beside Andy. She decided not to tell Andy who the bed belonged to right now. He seemed agitated enough already at having to stop.

The bedroom suite looked beautiful in Jordan's room and she loved it. Lisa helped her make the bed and decorate the room with her personal things. It was perfect.

Lisa's room was directly across the hall from Jordan's and she'd placed the dresser strategically so that she had full view of the room through the mirror. After all they'd been through with Heidi, Lisa had developed the "mother hen" syndrome. She had become over-protective of Jordan.

Andy and Jordan were watching a movie in the den while Heidi and Lisa lay on Lisa's bed discussing the details of Heidi's upcoming marriage to Aaron. Now that the move was out of the way, they could concentrate on more important things like the wedding dress, the cake and who would cater the food.

Heidi was so excited about her wedding that she rambled on and on, unaware that the bursitis in her mother's hips was giving her fits. Lisa kept turning as they talked, favoring one hip and then the other. When she turned to her left side she noticed movement in Jordan's room. She became aware of at least five orbs of light—shimmering, luminescent globes, as they materialized seemingly from the bed and began to float down the hallway directly toward them. Heidi, too, watched as the orbs of light stopped a mere three feet away from the foot of Lisa's bed. Seconds later, the manifestations began to dissolve.

Grabbing each other and holding on tightly, they realized they had unknowingly brought five souls into this house when they brought in Mr. Gordy's bed.

31

The House In the Country

The Wyricks were not actively looking for another house. They'd sold the Gordy furniture to a friend the same week Lisa and Heidi had seen the strange orbs floating from Jordan's room. Over the last few months they'd enjoyed sort of a freedom from constant anxiety and worry. They had no way of knowing that this was a transient condition.

Ester, Lisa's sister, just happened to mention a large house with acreage that was vacant. She knew the owner well. He'd moved to Florida and no one was living in the house. Ester thought he might be willing to rent it out if Lisa and Andy were interested. This house was a great deal larger than the duplex they were living in.

Lisa talked to Andy and they decided to check it out. They could certainly use the extra room.

The house was difficult to find. They'd traveled at least a quarter-mile down a dirt road before spotting the mailbox. They'd missed it several times. The long dirt driveway, not much wider than a pig trail, wound its way through the woods, the car bumping up and down as it hit potholes in the hard ground. The house, with an exterior of cedar, vertical board and batten siding, sat amidst tall Georgia pine trees nestled in nature.

"Ester said the door in the garage was supposed to be unlocked," Andy said, shoving the car in park. "Ya'll go on in. I'm gonna walk around back and take a look." Jordan got out of the car and caught up with him.

The garage floor was covered in red mud and garbage was piled up everywhere. Lisa and Heidi opened the door and walked through a small entryway that led into the kitchen.

"Honest-to-God, I believe this is the filthiest house I've ever seen," Lisa said disgustingly. "Look at these walls and this carpet. I don't even know if it could ever be cleaned up."

"Yeah, and look at this nasty stove." Heidi opened the oven door and closed it quickly.

"It would take some major time and cleaning just to get this place livable." Mold was growing around the air-conditioning vents. Red mud was caked in the tile grout.

Lisa and Heidi mounted a narrow staircase just inside the back door that led to an open loft. At the top of the steps there was a small, pigmy-like door held shut with a padlock.

"I wonder what that's for."

"I don't know. I'd like to get it open, though." Lisa pulled on the lock, then frowned when it didn't budge.

"It's probably nothing," Heidi said.

They looked around briefly before heading back downstairs.

Beyond the kitchen was the living area where a stone fireplace flanked one entire wall and carpet was in dire need of shampooing. The house was built on a slope; the backyard much lower than the front. There was a huge deck, at least 12 feet off the ground that overlooked a big back yard—a back yard surrounded by a thick forest of oaks, pines and sweet gums.

Lisa looked around. The place did have potential and she was up to the challenge, if a deal could be worked out with the owner.

Heidi walked through the rest of the house, scrutinizing every room. There was a long entry way coming through the front door. The master bedroom was on the right and two bedrooms on the left. She opened the door and looked out onto the narrow, concrete porch, it's roof being held up by three small posts. She closed the door and stood in the foyer. Something didn't feel right. A peculiar, eerie sensation crept over her, but she kept her comments to herself.

"I'm going outside with Daddy and Jordan," she said, making a quick exit through the back door. But as she covered the grounds with rapid strides, she turned and hurried back inside with her Momma. She'd felt the same thing outside as she had on the inside. The house and its surroundings were a pool of iniquity.

Jordan whooped and hollered as she and Andy scared some wildlife from its habitat. After a while they came in through the back door.

"Boy, I'd love to live out here in these woods." Andy was smiling. He'd already found a good spot to put up his deer stand.

"Look how nasty it is in here." Lisa shook her head. "You think we ought to ask about it?"

"I like the yard, but you're right, this place is a wreck." He looked around the kitchen, wiping his hand along the counter. "If you wanna clean this mess up, go ahead."

They struck a deal with the owner to clean and paint for the first month's rent. Lisa and Heidi painted and cleaned for weeks and by the time they got ready to move in, the house was as clean as it would ever get.

Heidi's furniture was in place and Lisa was helping her put sheets on the bed. "You've been awfully quiet Heidi. Is something wrong?"

"There's evil in this house, Momma, inside and outside. I can feel it."

Lisa was stunned. "How come you haven't said anything?"

"I don't know. I guess I didn't want to upset you. But I hate it here."

Lisa didn't know what to say.

The first two or three weeks in the house passed and Lisa had almost forgotten Heidi's warning. Then all hell broke loose.

A tropical storm off the Georgia/Florida coastline was causing storm warnings and flooding. Lisa had the television on listening for weather updates. Heidi and Jordan were sprawled out on the couch while Lisa finished up supper. Andy hadn't made it home yet.

Lightning zigzagged across the sky followed by a loud crack. The lights blinked off and on.

"Oh Lord, I hope we don't loose power," Lisa said from the kitchen. "Heidi, do you know where we put the candles?"

"Yeah, I'll get'em." Heidi opened a small drawer in the TV cabinet and pulled out four small candles and a book of matches. She sat them on the kitchen counter where they could be easily found in the dark.

After dinner, Heidi and Jordan cleaned the kitchen, then wandered off into their own rooms to get ready for bed. The lights flickered again.

Heidi's room felt cold. She pulled on a pair of thick socks, crawled in bed and picked up a book from the nightstand. She tried to read but the room was getting colder. She began to shiver and she knew, without seeing it, that something was in the room with her. The lights went off and didn't come back on. She lay in bed feeling extremely apprehensive.

Within seconds her feeling of dread turned physical. She felt cold hands wrap around her ankles—the chill penetrating her socks. Her body began to twist almost into a knot until she thought she heard her ribs crack. Her feet were being pulled upward toward the ceiling, her body folded, her neck bent. She fought like a wildcat to free herself, to no avail. Then lightning lit up the room and she could see the outline of a man—a man with a black suit and top hat. He moved between her and the horrible thing that attacked her. She felt the grip loosen from her ankles before plummeting downward to the bed.

When she was able, she began screaming for Lisa.

"What is it, Heidi?" Lisa was at the doorway.

"Momma, come get in bed with me. Please, Momma," She was crying.

"What on earth happened?"

Heidi couldn't explain it. "Please, just lay down with me."

Lisa slid under the sheets next to her. Heidi was trembling. "Stop crying and tell me what happened!"

"I can't. Not right now."

It was a while before the lights came back on and Heidi could explain.

The next night Lisa got in bed beside Heidi. She knew Heidi was still afraid and she began to talk about mundane things to keep her mind off last night. They both began to relax, to actually giggle as they talked about different family members and their humdrum existence, at least compared to theirs. Then suddenly the blanket between them began moving upward in a tent-like fashion, holding its position for a minute or so before it came back down to rest on the bed. Mixed emotions ran through them, emotions of reverence, dread and respect inspired by the power of the unknown.

"Heidi won't sleep by herself and I don't blame her," Lisa told Andy as they were getting ready for bed the next night. "I guess I'll have to sleep with her for a few more nights."

"If somebody's gotta sleep with her, it'll have to be you. I don't want to see nothin'. If I did see something, I'd be squallin' my tires outta here and I'd never come back!"

"That's what you always say," Lisa thought, *"and it's probably true."*

In grim despair they realized the years of torment they'd endured was never just *the house* on Swint Loop—*it was them! They were the magnets!*

Some people thought that the power of clairvoyance—the power to see and talk to the dead, was so strong in this family because the power of the mother and daughter consolidated and became twice as strong.

32

THE UNINVITED

Things began to worsen. Since Heidi was attacked the Wyricks had been awakened several times at night by sounds of footsteps stomping up and down the stairs that lead to the unused loft room. The stair treads weren't carpeted so they made a loud creaking noise when someone stepped on them, a sound loud enough that a profound sleeper would be awakened in any of the three bedrooms. Andy never caught anyone in the house and no clues were left behind that anyone had been there. Lisa equipped the stairs with pots, pans, dishes and piles of clothing. If the sounds were made by a human, she wanted to know it. If they weren't, she wanted to know that, too.

None of her booby traps were ever disturbed and yet the footsteps continued. Lisa toyed with the idea that someone might actually be living in the house with them. Maybe a vagrant was sleeping in the attic at night. That little padlocked door gave her the creeps. But if anyone ever jimmied the lock it would be obvious because of the poor condition of the hardware. She dismissed the thought.

Typically on Saturdays, Lisa and the girls ran errands in town while Andy went to his deer lease. Today was no different. In the afternoon they returned home with a trunk full of groceries. As she pulled into the drive, she noticed Andy's truck wasn't there yet. The dog was barking non-stop and she saw immediately that all the doors were wide open. She became alarmed.

"Both of ya'll sit right here while I check the house." She got out of the car and walked cautiously inside. Grabbing the portable telephone handset off the base, she dialed Joyce's number.

"Get out of the house, Lisa," Joyce advised, "and call the police." "I'm coming over there. Whatever you do, don't go back inside until I get there."

"Okay, I'll wait in the car." Lisa grabbed the wall phone from the hook and laid it on the kitchen counter, then backed out the door. She turned and ran straight for the car.

With the land line off the hook, Lisa and the kids listened. They could hear all kinds of racket going on in the house. It sounded like pots and pans rattling, dishes clattering, all kinds of different noises.

Lisa waited for Joyce, all the while listening to the strange noises through the phone. She would swear there were people in her house. She was parked where she could see all exits. If anybody left, she'd be sure to see them.

When Joyce arrived they went inside the house. Looking around, they found nothing out of order. They checked every room in the house and every nook and cranny where a person could hide. Everything was just as she left it this morning.

Checking beneath the counters she noticed none of her pots and pans out of place, her dishes stacked neatly in the cupboard. Everything was in order. Lisa was a neat freak. If anyone moved her stuff around she'd know it.

"Tell me this Lisa." Joyce looked her right in the eye. "What are ya'll *ever* gonna do?"

"Live the rest of our lives in torment, I guess," Lisa said, shrugging her shoulders "What else can we do?"

Lisa called the police and made out a report, but she wasn't hopeful they'd get to the bottom of it. She'd called the police many times but they couldn't help. She knew that. They'd lived this way for years and no one had been able to help. Outlandish and bizarre occurrences had become the norm, and never, never any answers.

She told Andy about it when he got home but he didn't have any suggestions, just that if he ever caught anybody he'd shoot first and ask questions later. That didn't help either. You couldn't shoot what you couldn't see.

Early Sunday morning Andy got up and went hunting. Lisa and Heidi were getting ready for church when they heard someone walking down the stairs. They were frightened. The footsteps were clear and concise. Lisa didn't doubt that somebody was there. She quietly woke Jordan, shushing her as they both ran quietly to Heidi's room, locking the door. Lisa lay flat on the floor watching through the gap beneath the closed door for any sign of movement. She saw nothing. Everything became so quiet you could've heard a pin drop before they emerged from Heidi's room.

If anybody *had* been in the house, they couldn't tell.

Lisa was reluctant to leave Heidi alone in the house that night but they had to go to her momma's, and besides, Heidi had a date. Aaron should be here shortly to take her to dinner.

Heidi wasn't about to let the latest family distress affect her date tonight with Aaron. He'd asked her to marry him and she'd accepted. The wedding date was set for June. That was only six months away. They had a lot to talk about.

She looked at herself critically in the freestanding full-length mirror in the corner of her room. She wore an indigo blue, linen dress—the edge of the bodice neatly trimmed with finely-woven cotton lace. Heidi had never been a flashy kind of person. She was genuine, there was no conceit or pretense about her and that added to her natural beauty. She turned this way and that and couldn't help but notice the cut of the dress was becoming to her. She'd purchased the dress as a part of her trousseau, but tonight was special and she decided to wear it.

She and Aaron were going out to dinner. He'd already told her that he had a surprise for her. She had her fingers crossed that it had to do with their honeymoon. He knew her dream of the perfect honeymoon had always been a mountain cabin—a place of blissful harmony between the two of them and nature.

"Oh, heck," Heidi said out loud. Her panty hose had a run right up the back. She looked at the clock. It was six-fifteen. She grabbed another pair and quickly put them on. She took one last look in the mirror to make sure everything was intact and made eye contact with the image of a man standing in the shadows just inside the front foyer. As her eyes focused in on him she could see that he was tall and thin. She shivered as she wondered how long he'd been watching her from behind. She called out "Daddy, is that you?" There was no answer. "Aaron?" Still there was no answer.

She didn't want to look in the mirror again but she knew she had to. The reflection was gone.

33

HEIDI'S PRIVATE NIGHTMARE

Heidi graduated from high school in May. Now she was working at a decent job and together with her Momma continued making plans for her wedding. Lying in bed she mulled over events throughout her school years. She speculated on just how cruel people could be and considered the fact that the spirit world had probably caused her less grief. She wasn't afraid of spirits. We would all be spirits one day. What she did fear was evil, both dead and alive and the way they could make your life a hell of unrelenting torment.

She'd had the esteemed honor of speaking at the commencement ceremony at her high school graduation. Her speech had been tough to write. There were so many things she hoped to forget and probably never would, and other things she'd like to remember forever. Some of the students she graduated with she'd gone to school with her whole life, and not many of them could she call friend. She'd suffered through ridicule, scorn and mockery ever since the first national television show aired her story. Just because she was different, some students had made it their personal goal to put her down. That goal would fail in more ways than one.

Her first year in middle school was probably the worst year of her life. Heidi had a naïve ignorance of life. She lacked worldliness and sophistication. She had a wide-eyed eager smile, a readiness to believe in people, to take them at face value. She had no earthly idea the world could be so cruel—no idea that her peers could be so heartless.

Mostly she kept the memories at bay, but tonight she allowed them to come flooding back. "Ooh, look. It's the little ghost girl." They all snickered. "Hey, ghost girl," one of them called out, "can you teach me how to cast a spell?" That brought loud cheers and laughter from around the room and began a barrage of insufferable comments.

Another girl stood to her feet and waved her arms in the air. "Boo, booooooo. I'm scared." Heidi was hurt to the core.

A calculated ploy to intimidate her manifested itself in verbal abuse, glowering threats or purposely embarrassing her, quickly creating a pecking order—the most powerful at the top, subordinates at the bottom. When events required choosing sides such as ball games during P.E. or class projects, Heidi would be last to be chosen. The teachers were just as guilty as they gave their tacit approval by condoning the behavior.

In the cafeteria, students wouldn't allow Heidi to sit down. They'd knock her books off the table or they'd spread out their legs in the empty chairs. Many times during lunch, she'd go into the bathroom stall with her Bible, just to sit and read. It was the only place she could find solace. That was until the teachers got a complaint and chastised Heidi, telling her the bathroom was off limits during lunch.

After church one Sunday, a group of teenagers invited her out. She was new there and thought this would be a great way to make friends. The girls that invited her must have had a preconceived plan to put Heidi in the front seat. Her long hair was pulled back into a ponytail and hung well below the top edge of the seat. The two girls in the back giggled and talked to each other, leaving her entirely out of the conversation. Something struck them as very funny but since she wasn't included in their joke, Heidi sat quietly as they rode. She'd smelled something burning at one point, but assumed they'd lit a cigarette and were smoking. Not until she got home and took her hair down, did she realize she'd been the reason they were laughing. The girls had singed the ends of her hair severely with the cigarette lighter.

Her heart felt heavy with tears and hurt. She felt as though the outside world hated her. She was constantly harassed and she couldn't remember anything she'd done to deserve it. She'd never been ugly to anyone, although she felt entitled to.

A letter came by mail addressed to her. "Heidi," it read, "My family and I went camping this weekend. We were sitting around the campfire having a good old time and guess who showed up? It was your friend, old man Gordy, of course. My momma went in the woods with him and he insisted they have sex. Just thought you'd want to know. Ghost watching is so much fun."

Heidi was devastated. To be cruel to her was one thing but there was no excuse for speaking evil of Mr. Gordy.

Heidi knew she was different and the fact was she shouldn't listen to them in the first place, because she always took it to heart. One day their cruel heartlessness would be dealt with—you reap what you sow.

When she entered high school things took a turn for the better. By the time she became a senior she had gained respect from other students, and more importantly, she'd gained the respect of her teachers.

Heidi, a girl who would never hurt anyone intentionally, had always been an honor student and who would eventually be inducted into the National Honor Society had been the recipient of spiteful, vicious teasing and name calling regarding events she had no control over. The old cliché, "what doesn't kill you will make you stronger," certainly applied here. This episode in Heidi's life only served to make her stronger, and she would need that strength for what was yet to come.

34

The Wedding

The day finally arrived that Heidi had anticipated since she was a little girl. It was her wedding day, the happiest day of a girl's life. Everything had turned out perfectly so far. Her search for the right bridal gown had taken her to Atlanta—at last choosing an elegant gown with a chapel train. The fit was perfect. The dress was sleeveless, made of white, matte satin—tiny pearls embedded in the bodice. Artistic patterns of jeweled sequins sparkled around the edge of her train—a diamond, teardrop necklace around her neck. The veil sat atop gorgeous dark curls; the rest of her hair hanging almost to her waist. She sat in the dressing room awaiting her cue.

As she waited, she wondered if Mr. Gordy was here, if he'd come to see her get married. She hoped so. She hadn't actually talked to him since she was eight years old but she'd always known he'd be there if she needed him. He'd watched her grow up; she knew that. He had been with her every step of the way. He'd kept watch over her, protected her over the years.

She knew a lot of people were deeply afraid of the supernatural. It was natural for adults to fear the unknown—to fear what they didn't understand. She didn't believe anyone truly comprehended the fact that Mr. Gordy was as real to her as they were.

She got a bicycle for Christmas that year she turned eight and her feet would barely reach the pedals. Her attempts to stay on were futile. Then, miraculously, as the bike started to waver, she felt someone behind her holding the bicycle steady. She turned, expecting to see her daddy, but it was Mr. Gordy. He was standing there holding the bicycle steady. He smiled at her and she smiled back. He gave her a push and she began to peddle furiously for the first time. She laughed out load as the wind caught her hair. She turned around to wave but he was gone. It was as if he was saying, *Okay, Heidi, you're on your own now. You can do it.* If she lived to be a hundred she'd never forget Mr. Gordy.

The bridesmaids had been given a dressing room that connected to hers. She could hear them laughing and talking in the other room. Her momma had stayed with her for a long time, helping her into her gown and veil. Now she'd left to take care of last-minute details in the church. Heidi was glad to have a few minutes to herself.

She walked over to the window and looked out. She could see Aaron's attendants down below but she couldn't see him. She felt like the luckiest person in the world. She sat down in a metal folding chair, thinking back on her life.

Con had lived next door to the house on Swint Loop more than fifty years ago and he, like Mr. Gordy, had visited her many times. But what really got under her skin was the little girl. She had wanted so badly to help her. She'd only seen her a few times and the girl never spoke, just looked at her with those sad eyes. She wondered what had happened to her, how she'd lost her life. Whatever business she'd had in this world, Heidi hoped it was resolved, that she had gone to a better place. She remembered the phrase that had entered her mind the first time she saw her, "*dressed for eternity.*" Heidi knew that people of all ages died. She knew that when God called, you had to go, no matter what your age. But there was something about children dying that she couldn't deal with.

She knew her family thought it was over, that she had outgrown her unnatural abilities, and she'd let them believe it. She was grown now and would handle it herself. She hadn't understood the consequences it had on her family then, both emotionally and physically, but she did now. Years of constant stress had caused her Momma to have a nervous disorder. She just hoped Aaron was fully aware of what he was committing to.

"Heidi?" Her daddy was knocking.

"Hey," she said. She could barely look at him.

"Man, don't you look pretty." She noticed his eyes were brimming with unshed tears.

He hugged her gently to keep from messing up her hair and makeup.

"You look good, too, Daddy," she said, "and you smell good."

He picked lint off his sleeve, then straightened his tie.

"Are you nervous?" She didn't have to ask.

"Does a mule have a tail?"

Heidi laughed.

Andy wanted his girls to be happy, but it was tearing his heart out to have to "give her away." It would be even harder if he didn't like Aaron so much.

"You make sure I do the right thing now, and don't' let me stumble over somethin'."

"Oh, Daddy, you'll be just fine." Heidi tried to ease his anxiety, but she felt a piece of her own heart tearing away.

Inside the church, Lisa sat alone in the pew, letting her nerves settle a little bit before the ceremony started. She'd been tearful since she opened her eyes this morning. When Lisa adjusted the wedding veil to make sure it hung properly, she'd suddenly remembered the day Heidi was born. How ironic, coming in to this world with a veil over her face and today, with a veil of a different sort, Lisa and Andy were giving her away in marriage.

Then memories of Heidi as a child flooded her mind: *the little girl playing the piano at her first recital, pounding out notes with little hands; running after Wolf, laughing. She was no longer a child. She was twenty years old and getting married. She'd led a complex, difficult, life, but had handled it well.* Lisa mopped her eyes with the tissue. It had been a rocky *road sometimes but they'd taken the rough with the smooth and come out ahead. Now here she was, making a leap into the adult world. Her little girl was grown up and leaving home. Lisa mopped her eyes again.*

Then she thought about the dark figure that haunted Heidi that caused so much turmoil in their life. Could it be that Heidi was being persecuted by the devil because of her unique relationship with God? If so, God prevailed and so did Heidi. She stood up against the principalities of darkness and triumphed. How many other people could say that?

Lisa was so deep in thought, when she looked up the church was already beginning to fill up. The music had started.

Heidi and Andy stood outside the church doors until they heard the familiar "Wedding March." They entered the church arm in arm. Everyone stood. Friends and family smiled as she walked down the isle. Heidi saw her sister, Jordan, standing at the altar. She looked beautiful and much older than ten. She saw her Momma and Memaw sitting close together on the front pew, both wiping their eyes. But when she looked up and saw Aaron, their eyes locked and at that moment no one else mattered.

Heidi and Aaron wrote their own vows, interchanging parts of the Bible with their own personal thoughts. Then the most romantic wedding event anybody had ever seen happened. Aaron took Heidi's hands, looked deep into her eyes and sang the most beautiful love song to her straight from his heart. There wasn't a dry eye in the church.

§

They spent a week in the Blue Ridge Mountains before returning home exhausted and blissfully happy. They retired early because Aaron had to go to work the next day and almost instantly he was out like a light. Heidi's mind was too full of activity to sleep. She went over and over all the details of the wedding, one by one reliving them. It was so glamorous, an absolute masterpiece. Heidi was giddy with happiness.

As she lay next to her sleeping husband she finally closed her eyes, still smiling.

Suddenly, her eyes blinked open and she found herself staring into the most piercing green eyes she'd ever seen.

Epilogue

Heidi stood in her grandparents' front yard on Swint Loop staring down the hill at the house next door; the house where she grew up. She was transported in time, reviving and reliving her childhood experiences, good and bad, in that house. Now there it sat once again, sad and neglected; weeds grown up around it, paint chipped off the shutters. Somewhere in the recesses of her mind she could hear familiar voices saying "get out of that house while you still can." Family members collectively blamed the house for all the illnesses the family suffered there and all the terror they were forced to bare witness to. It *was* curious that all of them had suffered life-threatening illnesses during the fifteen years they'd lived in that house. It was indeed strange, but the jury was still out on whether the house was guilty.

One thing was certain, Heidi thought, *there were ghosts in that house and ghosts that walked this land; wandering souls who hadn't moved on for one unique reason or another.* It was heart rendering. She'd never been blinded to these ghostly apparitions, not as a child, not now. Nor was she blinded to the perils she faced because of the ability she possessed. But was the house entirely at fault? Heidi thought not. Spirits were everywhere; not just at the house on Swint Loop.

From the moment of conception Heidi was sentenced to a life of painful consequences as a result of "the gift." The rules of nature were violated and she'd had to pay the penalty. Even in adulthood, Heidi still faces challenges and carries the burden brought on by the veil, but she and Aaron try to make the best of it, believing in the virtue of patience and prayer.

Being exposed to paranormal manifestations at such an early age, especially such a benign spirit as Mr. Gordy, allowed Heidi to normalize what the rest of us fear—the afterlife.

She sensed Aaron as he walked up behind her. He slipped an arm around her waist and stood silently beside her. She looked up at him and smiled.

"You ready to go eat? Your Nanny's got dinner on the table."

"Yeah, sure."

As they walked toward the house, hand in hand, her parent's pulled into the drive. They could see Jordan waving and smiling from the backseat. Clyde, their Jack Russell Terrier, bounded from the car as soon as the door cracked open. Heidi got down on her knees, rubbing his head laughing loudly at his antics. Wolf had died several years ago from dog fight wounds; he was doing what he always did—protecting the family. Although they loved Clyde, Wolf could never be replaced.

When Andy stepped from the car Heidi noticed how gray her Daddy's hair had gotten. He hugged her, averting his eyes from 'the house' as though to ward off any ill will it might project. If it wasn't for the fact that his parents lived here, he'd never ride down this road again.

Heidi waited for Lisa to get out of the car. They walked together up the back steps and on to the deck. They paused as they always did, trying to resist the urge to stare at the house down the hill.

A Note from the Authors

The title of this book came from an old wives tale regarding birth. Midwives have long spoken of certain babies born with a membrane covering their faces. The covering was referred to as a veil or caul. We now understand that a veil is part of the amnion, the inner membrane containing the fetus that sometimes remains intact after birth. This covering was thought to bring good luck and was sometimes preserved and kept by its owner. A veil was also thought to have special powers that would keep one from drowning, and therefore highly sought after by sailors and would bring large sums of money.

According to these ancient tales, people born with this veil had extrasensory perception and could see things not visible to ordinary people, such as visions and spirits. However, there is more to being born with a veil than mere superstition. Such historical figures as Charles Dickens and Alexander the Great were said to have been born with a veil and able to see beyond the realm of reality as we know it. Research shows this phenomenon is rare and, in most cases, these babies are born prematurely.

Heidi Wyrick is such a person. She was called a "miracle child" from birth because she beat all odds of living. She was born a month early with the umbilical cord wrapped twice around her neck, cutting off the blood flow to her brain. Not only did she beat the odds, she is also very astute. She excelled in high school and scored in the top five percentile on her SAT tests.

Heidi has the capacity to discern, connect and interact with those who preceded us in death. Others have similar capabilities, but there is one particular distinction. Not only does she communicate verbally with the dead, she is also able to identify them. Heidi's rare abilities became obvious when she was very young, and even at the age of twenty-one she continues seeing things others can't discern. We're left to wonder why certain people are endowed with such an extraordinary talent. Her life will forever be unique as she faces challenges caused by her ability to perhaps go backward in time—a place called the fourth dimension.

978-0-595-42115-2
0-595-42115-6

Printed in the United States
77677LV00004B/124